JEWISH
FIRST
NAMES

HIPPOCRENE BOOKS
New York

JEWISH
FIRST
NAMES

David C. Gross

Front Cover: Micah Williams, *Girl in White with Cherries* oil on canvas, 1831. Used by permission of the Jane Voorhees Zimmerli Art Museum, Rutgers, The State University of New Jersey, Gift of Anna I. Morgan.

ISBN 0-7818-0727-1

For information, address:
HIPPOCRENE BOOKS, INC.
171 Madison Avenue
New York, NY 10016

Printed in the United States of America

For Gabriel Judah

Contents

Preface
ix

■ ■ ■

Girls' Names
1

■ ■ ■

Boys' Names
55

*"Every person has three names—
one that his parents gave him,
one others call him, and one he acquires himself."*

—ECCLESIASTES

Preface

To give a name to a newborn infant is a joyous occasion. It is also a great challenge and responsibility. In most Jewish families, but nowadays not in all, a child is named in memory of a beloved relative. The choice of a name is very often a conscious, or at time unconscious, linking of the new child to nearly four thousand years of Jewish history. Memorializing a deceased relative or friend is usually a custom in Ashkenazic families; in the Sephardic tradition, it is acceptable to name a child after a living relative. In Israel, where a large number of people are descendants of survivors of the Holocaust, there is a strong desire to link a new baby to a victim of the Holocaust— for in Jewish tradition, the erasing of a name and its memory is a curse. Another powerful influence in naming a child in Israel is the wish to link the newborn to ancient roots—thus, many young Israelis bear the names of little-known biblical figures, as well as indigenous flowers, trees, mountains and regions.

Until very recently, the vast majority of Jewish infants bore traditional biblical names such as *Abraham, Isaac, Jacob, Joseph, David, Sarah, Rebecca, Leah, Rachel, Esther*. But even these traditional names varied from country to country. For example, first cousins named for the same beloved grandfather might be named *Ezekiel* in America, *Jorge* in Argentina, and *Chesta* in Israel.

Like clothing, music, art, and so many other areas of life, names too are either "in" or not; they also, it seems, run in cycles. When the first Jewish immigrants landed on American shores, their newborn infants tended to be named *Jake, Max, Sam, Hyman, Fanny, Molly* or *Sadie*. That was at the beginning of the twentieth century; now, roughly four generations later, it

is no longer surprising to hear new Jewish infant boys being designated these names again. Most new mothers and fathers, however, still wish to memorialize a beloved parent or grandparent or other relative. At the turn of the millennium, a family may not however wish to name a daughter *Goldie*, deeming it too old-fashioned. What to do? Since a Jewish child generally has a Hebrew name and an English name, the solution is simply to keep the original name in Hebrew, but the English name—which the child will use most of the time—retains the first letter of the decedent being memorialized. Thus, the little girl may be known as *Ginger*.

As is generally known, in the Jewish community infant boys are usually named at the time of their circumcision. When a male Jewish child is born, it is customary to have a circumcision ceremony on the eighth day following the birth (the day of birth is counted). This ruling is relaxed if there is a medical reason to do so. Part of the Bris or Brit ceremony is the announcement of the boy's name. Thus, parents should decide on the name prior to the ceremony. A *mohel* (in Yiddish *moil*) is the ritual circumciser. The overwhelming majority are highly experienced, and the circumcision generally is over in a matter of moments. The circumcision ceremony is an affirmation of the covenant between God and Abraham, i.e., the Jewish people, that dates back nearly three and a half thousand years.

When a female Jewish child is born, it is customary to name the infant in the synagogue, at Sabbath services, during the weekly reading of the Torah. The rabbi reads aloud the appropriate prayer, names the child, and the congregation responds with a resounding "Mazel Tov." A collation at the family home, or in the synagogue, or both, usually follows.

In the Jewish community, names are truly important. An ancient sage, Simeon bar Yochai, taught that there are three

crowns—royalty, priesthood, and the Torah. And the crown of a good name is superior to them all, he said. Judaism teaches that a good name is more valuable than precious oil.

I know of one family—there are certainly many others—where a son was especially desirable, for there were many daughters but only one son. He was named *Zaida*, meaning grandpa in Yiddish, in the hope that he would have a long life. A century or two ago, Jewish boys born on Passover or another holiday were often named *Pesah* (the Hebrew word for Passover) or *Yomtov* ("holiday" in Hebrew). If a man is critically ill, he is renamed *Chayim* ("life" in Hebrew), in the hope that this will help him recover. A desperately sick woman is renamed *Chaya*, the feminine equivalent.

There are some 1,300 Jewish first names for boys and girls in this book. They trace their origins to Hebrew, Yiddish, Aramaic, and various European languages. The sources of the names are biblical, talmudic, historic, modern Israeli, and contemporary. Every name is identified and its meaning explained; popular nicknames are included.

A recent phenomenon is the creation of new names. A baby girl named for a deceased *David* is designated *Davida* or *Davidine*. A girl being named for two deceased women, *Erica* and, *Ellen*, emerges with a brand-new name, *Eren*. Names that many believe to be Jewish in origin are not, although they may sound it. For example, *Ida* used to be very popular name; it is originally Old Norse.

Under all circumstances, naming a new child is a beautiful, joyous, challenging and responsible task. Good luck—and Mazel Tov!

—D.C.G.

Pronunciation Note

The *ch* in this book is pronounced like the *ch* in the Scottish pronunciation of "loch."

Many names that begin with *j* or *y* are usually pronounced with a *y* sound. For example, *Jochanan* and *Yochanan*.

Girls' Names

𝕬

Abbe Diminutive names for *Abigail*. Variant: *Abby*.

Abibi Variant spelling for *Aviva*.

Abigail From Hebrew, meaning "father's joy." Following the death of her husband, Nabal, the Bible mentions her as King David's wife. Nickname: *Gail*.

Abiela From Hebrew, meaning "God is my father." Variant spelling: *Aviela*.

Abira From Hebrew, meaning "strong."

Abital Variant spelling of *Avital*, meaning "father of dew" in Hebrew. In the Bible she was one of King David's wives. A popular nickname is *Tali*.

Ada From Hebrew, meaning "ornament." Ada is listed in the Bible as the wife of Esau.

1

Adamina Coined in Scotland as a feminine version of Adam. Now seldom used.

Adiella From Hebrew, meaning "God's ornament." Nicknames: *Adele, Adeline*.

Adina From Hebrew, meaning "noble, pleasant, delicate."

Aderet From Hebrew, meaning "cape" or "outer garment."

Adira From Hebrew, meaning "mighty."

Adiva From Hebrew, meaning "pleasant, gracious."

Adiya From Hebrew, meaning "God's treasure."

Adoniah From Hebrew, meaning "my Lord is God." Mentioned in the Bible. Also said to be a Greek, feminine form of Adonis, hence meaning "beautiful lady."

Adva From Aramaic, meaning "wave" or "ripple."

Afra From Hebrew, meaning "young, female deer." Variant spelling: *Ofra*.

Aharona Feminine form of Aharon (Aaron), Moses' brother.

Ahuda From Hebrew, meaning "adored."

Ahuva From Hebrew, meaning "beloved." Variant: *Ahuviya*.

Aleeza From Hebrew, meaning "joyous one."

Alexandra From Greek, meaning "helper of mankind." Queen Salome Alexandra, who ruled Judea for a decade, was one of the first women to adopt this name. Diminutives include *Sandra* and *Alexa*.

Alita From Hebrew, meaning "high, excellent."

Alitza From Hebrew, meaning "happiness."

Aliyah From Hebrew, meaning "ascension."

Alma From Hebrew, meaning "maiden."

Alona From Hebrew, meaning "oak tree." Feminine form of the popular boys' name, Alon.

Alufa From Hebrew, meaning "princess" or "leader."

Aluma From Hebrew, meaning "girl" or "secret."

Amalya From Hebrew, meaning "the Lord's work."

Amana From Hebrew, meaning "faithful."

Amela From Hebrew, meaning "industrious."

Ami From Hebrew, meaning "my people."

Amina From Hebrew, meaning "trusted."

Amira From Hebrew, meaning "speech."

3

Amit From Hebrew, meaning "honest, trustful." Variant: *Amita*.

Amitza From Hebrew, meaning "strong" or "brave."

Anat From Hebrew, meaning "to sing." In the Bible it is oddly a man's name; the Talmud describes it as a bird.

Ann, Anne, Anita All variants of the Hebrew name *Hannah*, found in the Bible, meaning "merciful, gracious." Nicknames include *Nancy, Nanette,* and *Nita*.

Arela From Hebrew, meaning "angel" or "messenger."

Ariel From Hebrew, meaning "lioness of God." Variant: *Ariela*.

Ariza From Hebrew, meaning "cedar beams." Variant: *Arza*.

Armona From Hebrew, meaning "castle."

Arnon From Hebrew, meaning "roaring stream."

Ashera From Hebrew, meaning "contented."

Ashira From Hebrew, meaning "wealthy one."

Asisa From Hebrew, meaning "juicy."

Asisya From Hebrew, meaning "juice of the Lord."

Astera A Hebraized version of the Aster flower; related to the biblical name *Esther*. Usually translated as a star-flower.

Atalya From Hebrew, meaning "God is exalted." Also from Aramaic.

Atara From Hebrew, meaning "crown" or "wreath." Variant: *Ateret*.

Atida From Hebrew, meaning "the future."

Atira From Hebrew, meaning "prayer."

Atura From Hebrew, meaning "ornamented."

Atzila From Hebrew, meaning "noble."

Ava From Hebrew, meaning "desire." Possibly also from Latin, designating a bird.

Aviella From Hebrew, meaning "God is my father."

Avigal From Hebrew, meaning "father's joy." Variant: *Avigayil*.

Avigdora Feminine form of the Hebrew name Avigdor, meaning "father's protector."

Avirit From Hebrew, meaning "spirit" or "air."

Aviva From Hebrew, meaning "springtime." Variant spelling: *Haviva*.

Avivi From Hebrew, meaning "spring-like."

Avinoam From Hebrew, meaning "father of delight." This was the name of one of King David's wives; it is also used for boys.

Avna From Hebrew, meaning "stone."

Avuka From Hebrew, meaning "torch."

Aya From Hebrew, meaning "to fly swiftly."

Ayala From Hebrew, meaning "gazelle." Variant: *Ayelet*.

Aza From Hebrew, meaning "powerful."

Aziza From Hebrew, meaning "strong."

𝕭

Baila From Yiddish, meaning "white." Possibly related to one of Jacob's concubines, *Bilha*.

Balfouria Feminine form of the name Balfour, a recently-coined name honoring the British statesman, Lord Balfour, whose efforts for a Jewish homeland led to the creation of the State of Israel.

Bara From Hebrew, meaning "to choose."

Basya From Yiddish, meaning "daughter of God." Hebrew version: *Batya*. Nickname: *Basha*.

Bathsheba From Hebrew, meaning "daughter of an oath." Bathsheba was King Solomon's mother and King David's favorite wife. Variant spelling: *Batsheba*.

Bat-Shir From Hebrew, meaning "songbird."

Bat-Tsiyon From Hebrew, meaning "daughter of Zion."

Bat-Yam From Hebrew, meaning "daughter of the sea."

Behira From Hebrew, meaning "bright, brilliant."

Benyamina Feminine form of the Hebrew name Benyamin, meaning "son of my right hand."

Berucha From Hebrew, meaning "blessed." Variant: *Beruchiya*, meaning "blessed of God."

Beruriah From Hebrew. The only woman talmudic scholar recognized and admired by her male colleagues. The name is usually translated as "pure."

Betuel From Hebrew, meaning "daughter of God."

Beulah From Hebrew, meaning "married."

Bina From Hebrew, meaning "understanding" and "wisdom."

Bira From Hebrew, meaning "capital" or "fortified city."

Bluma From Yiddish, meaning "flower." Variant spelling: *Blume*.

Booba From Hebrew, meaning "doll."

Bracha From Hebrew, meaning "a blessing."

Bruna From Yiddish, meaning "brunette." Variants: *Brina, Breindel*.

ℭ

Carmel From Hebrew, meaning "vineyard." Variant: *Carmela, Carmen*. Nickname: *Carmi*.

Carna From Aramaic, meaning "horn" (of an animal) or "strength." Variant: *Carnit*.

Carniya From Hebrew, meaning "horn of God."

Chagit From Aramaic, meaning "festive celebration."

Chagigya From Hebrew, meaning "God's festival."

Chamuda From Hebrew, meaning "loved one."

Chana From Hebrew, meaning "gracious, merciful." Variant spelling: *Hannah*.

Chasida From Hebrew, meaning "righteous woman." Yiddish equivalent: *Fruma*. Also translates as "stork."

Chasina From Aramaic, meaning "strong." Variant: *Chasna*.

Chava From Hebrew, meaning "life." The biblical form of *Eve*.

Chaviva From Hebrew, meaning "beloved, sweetie."

Chaya From Hebrew, meaning "life."

Cheftziba From Hebrew, meaning "she is my desire."

Chemda From Hebrew, meaning "charming."

Chita From Hebrew and Aramaic, meaning "grain" or "wheat."

Coral From Hebrew and Greek, meaning "small stone."

Dafnit Hebrew equivalent of the Greek name Daphne, meaning "laurel."

Dagania From Hebrew, meaning "corn" or "grain." Variant: *Degania*.

Dalgiya From Hebrew, meaning "rope."

Dalia From Hebrew, meaning "to draw water" or "a branch." Variant: *Dalit*.

Dana Feminine form of the Hebrew name Dan, meaning "she judges."

Daniela Feminine form of the Hebrew name Daniel, meaning "God is my judge." Variants: *Danielle*, *Danit*.

Danya From Hebrew, meaning "God's judgment."

Daroma From Hebrew, meaning "southward."

Darona From Hebrew, meaning "gift." Variant spelling: *Dorona*.

Dasa Nickname for *Hadassah*. Variant: *Dasi*.

Datya From Hebrew, meaning "faith in God." Variant spelling: *Datiya*.

Davene Feminine form David, meaning "beloved." Variants: *Davida*, *Davidine*.

Daya From Hebrew, meaning "bird of prey."

Deborah From Hebrew *D'vora*, a woman judge mentioned in the Bible. Meaning also "swarm of bees" or "speaking kind words." Variant: *Debra*. Nickname: *Debbie*.

Degula From Hebrew, meaning "famous, honored."

Derora From Hebrew, meaning "freedom."

Deu'ela From Hebrew, meaning "knowledge of the Lord."

Devash From Hebrew, meaning "honey." Variant: *Devasha*.

Devoranit From Hebrew, designating a variety of orchid.

Digla From Hebrew, meaning "a flag."

Dikla From Aramaic, meaning "palm tree."

Dinah From Hebrew, meaning "judgment."

Disa From Yiddish. Nickname for *Judith* (*Yehudit* in Yiddish).

Ditza From Hebrew, meaning "joy."

Doda From Hebrew, meaning "beloved" or "aunt."

Dodi From Hebrew, meaning "my beloved."

Dorit From Hebrew, meaning "generation."

Dorya From Hebrew, meaning "generation of God." Variant spelling: *Doria*.

Doveva From Hebrew, meaning "graceful." Variants: *Dova*, *Dovit*.

Dovrat From Hebrew. A variant of *Deborah*.

Duba From Hebrew, meaning "female bear."

Dushe From Yiddish. A nickname form of *Deborah*.

Duvsha From Aramaic, meaning "honey."

D'voshka From Yiddish. A nickname form of *Deborah*.

Edel From Yiddish, meaning "gentle, refined." Variant: *Eidel*.

Eder From Hebrew, meaning "flock" or "herd."

Edna From Hebrew, meaning "delightful" or "adorned." The name is mentioned in the Apocrypha, the Book of Tobit.

Edya From Hebrew, meaning "God's adornment."

Efrat From Hebrew, meaning "fruitful" or "distinguished." Variant: *Efrata*.

Efrona From Hebrew, meaning "bird."

Eifa From Hebrew, meaning "darkness." In the Bible, Caleb's concubine.

Eila From Hebrew, meaning "oak" or "terebinth tree."

Eilat From Hebrew, meaning "gazelle" or "tree." Listed in the Bible in the time of the Judean kingdom. Today it is the name of Israel's southernmost city.

Elana Variant spelling of *Ilana*.

Eliana From Hebrew, meaning "my God has answered."

Eliava From Hebrew, meaning "my God is willing."

Eli'ezra Feminine form of the Hebrew name Eliezer, meaning "my God is salvation."

Elinoar From Hebrew, meaning "God is my youth."

Eliora From Hebrew, meaning "my God is light."

Eliraz From Hebrew, meaning "my God is (my) secret."

Elisheva From Hebrew, meaning "God's oath." Akin to *Elizabeth*.

Elona From Hebrew, meaning "oak tree." Variant spelling: *Alona*.

Elula Feminine form of the Hebrew name Elul, meaning a Jewish calendar month.

Elza From Hebrew, meaning "joy."

Emanuela Feminine form of the Hebrew name Emanuel, meaning "God is with us."

Emet From Hebrew, meaning "truth."

Emunah From Hebrew, meaning "faith."

Erana From Hebrew, meaning "industrious, energetic."

Erela From Hebrew, meaning "angel."

Eretz From Hebrew, meaning "country, land."

Esther From Persian. Usually translated into Hebrew as *Hadassah*, meaning "myrtle." Heroic queen after whom a biblical book is named, and whose saving of the Jewish people is celebrated at Purim. Nicknames: *Essie, Essa, Etty.*

Etana From Hebrew, meaning "strong." Variant spelling: *Aytana.*

Etka From Yiddish. Nickname for *Itta* and *Yetta.*

Eve English form of *Chava.* Adam's wife in the Bible.

Evrona From Hebrew, meaning "rage." Variant: *Avrona.*

Ezraela Feminine form the of the name Ezra. From Hebrew, meaning "God is my support."

Faiga From Yiddish, meaning "bird." Variant: *Faigel*.

Fraydel From Yiddish, meaning "joy." Variant spellings: *Fraidel, Frayda*.

Fruma From Yiddish, meaning "pious woman." Variant spelling: *Frume*.

G

Ga'alya From Hebrew, meaning "God has redeemed."

Gabriella From Hebrew, meaning "God is my strength." Variant: *Gabrielle*. Nickname: *Gabi*.

Gada Feminine form of Gad, one of Jacob's twelve sons.

Gadiela From Hebrew, meaning "God is my good fortune."

Gafna From Aramaic, meaning "vine." Variant: *Gafnit*.

Gal From Hebrew, meaning "a wave," "fountain" or "hill."

Galila From Hebrew, meaning "roll away."

Galiya From Hebrew, meaning "hill of God." Variant: *Galya*.

15

Gamliela Feminine form of the Hebrew name Gamliel, meaning "God is my reward."

Gana From Hebrew, meaning "garden." Variant: *Ganit.*

Ganya From Hebrew, meaning "the Lord's garden."

Gat From Hebrew, meaning "wine press."

Gayora From Hebrew, meaning "valley of light."

Gazit From Hebrew, meaning "hewn stone."

Ge'ona From Hebrew, meaning "wisdom."

Gershona Feminine version of the Hebrew name Gershon, meaning "stranger."

Geula From Hebrew, meaning "redemption."

Gevionit From Hebrew, meaning "lilac."

Gevira From Hebrew, meaning "lady" or "queen."

Gevura From Hebrew, meaning "heroism" or "strength." Related name: *Gibora*, meaning "heroine."

Gideona Feminine form of the Hebrew name Gideon, meaning "great warrior."

Gila From Hebrew, meaning "joy." Variants: *Gil, Gili.*

Gilada From Hebrew, meaning "joy is forever." Variants: *Gilana, Gilit.*

Gili From Hebrew, meaning "my joy."

Giliya From Hebrew, meaning "my joy is in the Lord."

Gina From Hebrew, meaning "garden." Variant: *Ginat.*

Gittel From Yiddish, meaning "good." Nickname: *Gitti.*

Giva From Hebrew, meaning "high place" or "hill." Variant: *Givona.*

Givola From Hebrew, meaning "bird."

Glucke From Yiddish, meaning "good luck." Nickname: *Gluckel, Glickel.*

Golda From Yiddish, meaning "golden." Nicknames: *Goldie, Goldarina.*

Gomer From Hebrew, meaning "to complete, to finish." Also a boy's name.

Gozala From Hebrew, meaning "young bird."

Gurit From Hebrew, meaning "young lion."

H

Hadar From Hebrew, meaning "ornamented, beautiful." Another meaning is "glory." Variant: *Hadara*.

Hadassah From Hebrew, meaning "myrtle tree," symbolizing victory. In the Bible's Book of Esther, she is alluded to by her Hebrew name, Hadassah. Nicknames: *Dasi* and Yiddish *Hodel*.

Hamuda From Hebrew, meaning "desirable" or "precious." Alternative spelling: *Chamuda*.

Haniya From Hebrew, meaning "a resting place."

Hannah Variant spelling of the Hebrew name *Chana*, meaning "gracious, merciful."

Harela Feminine form of the Hebrew name Harel, meaning "mountain of God."

Hasya From Hebrew, meaning "protected by the Lord."

Hedia From Hebrew, meaning "voice of the Lord." Variant: *Hedya*.

Hedva From Hebrew, meaning "joy."

Hende A Yiddish version of *Hannah*. Variant: *Hennie*.

Hertzela A feminine form of the Hebrew name Herzl, a name popularized in recent years honoring Theodor Herzl, founder of the Zionist movement. Variant: *Herzliah*.

Hila From Hebrew, meaning "praise." Also the feminine form of Hillel. Variant spelling: *Chila*. Variant: *Chilana*.

Hillela Feminine form of the Hebrew name Hillel, meaning "the shining one" or "praised." Nickname: *Hili*.

Hinda From Yiddish, meaning "deer." Diminutive: *Hindie*.

Hodiya From Hebrew, "praise the Lord" or "God is my splendor." The name is found in the Bible.

Horiah From Hebrew, meaning "God's teaching."

Hula From Hebrew, meaning "to play (an instrument)."

Hulda From Hebrew, meaning "to dig." This was the name of a prophetess in King Josiah's time.

I

Idit From Yiddish, nickname form of *Judith* (*Yehudit* in Hebrew).

Idra From Aramaic, meaning "fig tree." Historically, it symbolized great scholarship.

Idria From Hebrew, meaning "duck."

Ilana From Hebrew, meaning "tree." Variant: *Ilanit*.

Ilit From Aramaic, meaning "superlative." Variant: *Ila*.

Imanuella Variant spelling of *Emanuella*, feminine form of Emanuel.

Ima From Hebrew, meaning "mother." Variant: *Imma*.

Inbal From Hebrew, meaning "a bell clapper."

Irit From Hebrew, meaning "a plant of the lilac family."

Isaaca Feminine form of Isaac (*Yitzhak* in Hebrew), meaning "he will laugh."

Itai From Aramaic, meaning "timely."

Iti From Hebrew, meaning "with me."

Itiel From Hebrew, meaning "God is with me." Variant: *Itiya*.

Ivrit From Hebrew, meaning "the Hebrew language." Variant: *Ivrita*.

Ivriya Feminine form of the Hebrew name Ivri, meaning "a Hebrew (person)."

J

Jacoba Feminine form of the Hebrew name Jacob, meaning "held by the heel." Nicknames: *Jackie*. Variant: *Jacobina*.

Jael From Hebrew, meaning "to ascend." Variant spelling: *Yael*.

Jasmina From Hebrew, meaning "jasmine." Variant: *Jasmine*.

Jemina From Hebrew, meaning "right-handed."

Jennifer From Hebrew and Latin, meaning "graceful bearing."

Jessica From Hebrew, meaning "God's grace." Nickname: *Jessie*.

Jethra Feminine form of the Hebrew name Jethro, meaning "in abundance." He was Moses' father-in-law.

Jocheved From Hebrew, the name of Moses' mother. Variant spelling: *Yocheved*.

Joela Feminine form of the Hebrew name Joel, meaning "God is willing." A minor prophet in the Bible.

Johanna The feminine equivalent of the Hebrew boys' name Yochanan, usually translated as "gracious." The name is related to *Hannah*.

Jonah From Hebrew, name of the biblical prophet Jonah, meaning "dove." Used for boys and girls.

Jonina From Hebrew, meaning "dove." Variants: *Jonit*, *Jonati*.

Jordana English form of the Hebrew name *Yardena*, meaning "flowing down." Nickname: *Jordie*.

Judith English form of the Hebrew name *Yehudit*, meaning "praise." Judith was a great heroine in biblical history. Nicknames: *Judy, Jody*.

𝕶

Kadisha From Hebrew, meaning "holy."

Kadiya From Hebrew, meaning "pitcher."

Kalanit Israeli name of a colorful, popular flower.

Kama From Hebrew, meaning "ripened grain."

Kanara From Hebrew, meaning "harpist" or "canary."

Kanit From Hebrew, meaning "songbird."

Karmil From Hebrew, meaning "crimson."

Karna From Hebrew, meaning "horn (of an animal)."

Karniela From Hebrew, meaning "the Lord's horn."

Kaspit From Hebrew, meaning "silver."

Kataniya From Hebrew, meaning "very small."

Kedma From Hebrew, meaning "eastward."

Kelila From Hebrew, meaning "crown" or "laurel," which are both symbols of beauty.

Keret From Hebrew, meaning "city" or "settlement."

Keshet From Hebrew, meaning "rainbow" or "arc."

Keshisha From Aramaic, meaning "elderly lady."

Keshuva From Hebrew, meaning "attentive."

Ketzia From Hebrew, meaning "related to fragrance." Also one of Job's daughters.

Kida From Hebrew, designating a plant that, during Temple days, produced a spice added to the sacred oil.

Kinneret From Hebrew, meaning "harp." The Hebrew name of Israel's largest lake, Lake Tiberias.

Kitron From Hebrew, meaning "crown."

Kochava From Hebrew, meaning "Aster." Variant: *Kochavit*.

Kolya From Hebrew, meaning "God's voice."

Koranit From Hebrew, meaning "thistle."

Korenet From Hebrew, meaning "shining."

Kreindel From Yiddish, meaning "crown." Variant: *Kreine*.

L

Laila From Hebrew, meaning "night." Variants: *Laylie, Laili*.

Latifa From Hebrew, meaning "a caress."

Layish From Hebrew, meaning "lion." Also a boys' name.

Leah From Hebrew, meaning "to be tired." Name of Jacob's first wife in the Bible.

Leeba From Yiddish, meaning "beloved." In modern Hebrew, translated as "her heart."

Lena From Hebrew, meaning "to dwell" or "a residence."

Le'ora From Hebrew, meaning "toward the light." Variant: *Le'orit.*

Leron From Hebrew, meaning "the song is mine." Also a boy's name.

Levana From Hebrew, meaning "moon" or "white."

Levia From Hebrew, meaning "to join up." Also the feminine form of Levi, meaning "joined to."

Leviva From Hebrew, meaning "pancake."

Levona From Hebrew, meaning "incense" or "spice."

Lilach From Persian, meaning "lilac." Nickname: *Lea.*

Lirit From Hebrew, meaning "musical, lyrical."

Lital From Hebrew, meaning "the dew is mine."

Le'uma From Hebrew, meaning "nation."

M

Ma'anit From Hebrew, meaning "frame" or "marker."

Ma'ayan From Hebrew, meaning "fountain." Variant: *Ma'ayana*.

Machla From Hebrew, meaning "stocky, fat." In the Bible, a daughter of Zelophechad.

Magena From Hebrew, meaning "protector." Variant: *Magina*.

Mehira From Hebrew, meaning "swift, energetic."

Maya Of Roman origin. Although this name stems from Roman mythology and refers to the goddess of earth, it is used in Israel today.

Makabit The feminine form of the Hebrew name Maccabee. The name is an acronym meaning "Who Is Like Thee, O God," featured in the Hanukkah festival.

Makeda From Hebrew, meaning "cup" or "bowl." A place name in the Bible.

Maksima From Hebrew, meaning "enchanting" or "miracle performer." Variant spelling: *Maxima*.

Malach From Hebrew, meaning "angel." Used also for boys.

Malbina From Hebrew, meaning "to whiten" or "to embarrass."

Malka From Hebrew, meaning "queen." Variant: *Malkiya*.

Malkosha From Hebrew, meaning "last rain of the year."

Mana From Hebrew, meaning "a portion." Variants: *Mania, Menat*.

Manachat From Hebrew, meaning "restfulness."

Mangina From Hebrew, meaning "melody."

Ma'or From Hebrew, meaning "light." Boys and girls born during the Chanukah season are often given this name.

Margalit From Greek, meaning "a pearl." Popular Israeli name. Variant: *Margalita*.

Marganit Hebrew name of a colorful plant growing in Israel. Variant: *Marganita*.

Marina From Latin, meaning "from the sea." Popular girls' name in Israel, brought in by Russian immigrants.

Marta From Aramaic, meaning "sorrowful." Nicknames: *Marda, Marita*.

Marva From Hebrew, designating a plant in the mint family.

Mari'ashe A Yiddish form of Miriam, meaning "sea of sorrow."

Masada From Hebrew, originally *Metzada*, meaning "foundation" or "support."

Mas'eit From Hebrew, meaning "gift."

Mashena From Hebrew, meaning "resting place."

Maskit From Hebrew, meaning "a portrait" or "engraving."

Masu'a From Hebrew, meaning "a signal" or "torch."

Matama From Hebrew, meaning "delicacy."

Matana From Hebrew, meaning "gift." Variants: *Matat, Mat'nat.*

Mat'konet From Hebrew, meaning "a measure" or "a format."

Matmona From Hebrew, meaning "treasure."

Matred From Hebrew, meaning "continue without interruption." This name is mentioned in the Bible.

Matzhelet From Hebrew, meaning "shout of joy."

Matzila From Hebrew, meaning "rescuer, savior."

Mazal From Hebrew, meaning "luck." A popular Sephardic name. Variant: *Mazalit.*

Mazhira From Hebrew, meaning "shining."

Mechola From Hebrew, meaning "a dance."

Mechubada From Hebrew, meaning "honored, respected."

Medina From Hebrew, meaning "country."

Me'ira Feminine form of the Hebrew name Meir, meaning "bringing light."

Meirona From Aramaic, meaning "sheep." Also from Hebrew, meaning "troops."

Meital From Hebrew, meaning "dew drops."

Meitar From Hebrew, meaning "string" or "cord."

Melabevet From Hebrew, meaning "endearing."

Menachema Feminine form of the Hebrew name Menachem, meaning "comfort." Variant: *Menachemiya*.

Menorah From Hebrew, meaning "candelabrum."

Menucha From Hebrew, meaning "peace, rest."

Meirav From Hebrew, meaning "warrior" or "to increase." This was the name of King Saul's eldest daughter. Variant spelling: *Merav*.

Me'ona From Hebrew, meaning "a dwelling place," referring usually to the temple.

Me'ora From Hebrew, meaning "light."

Merchavia From Hebrew, meaning "God's space."

Meri From Hebrew, meaning "rebellious." Variant spelling" *Merrie*.

Merima From Hebrew, meaning "raised up."

Meroma From Hebrew, meaning "noble, high."

Meshulemet From Hebrew, meaning "complete" or "peaceful." King Manassah's wife in the Bible.

Me'usheret From Hebrew, meaning "blessed" or "contented."

Me'uzah From Hebrew, meaning "strength."

Mevorechet From Hebrew, meaning "blessed."

Michal Feminine form of Michael, meaning "who is like God." This was the name of King Saul's daughter, the wife of David. Variants: *Michaela*, *Michelle*.

Michayahu From Hebrew, a variant of *Michal*. In the Bible, she was the wife of Rehoboam, king of Judah.

Mifrach From Hebrew, meaning "flight." Variant: *Mifrachat*.

Migda From Hebrew, meaning "a choice thing" or "gift." Variant: *Migdana*.

Milet From Hebrew, meaning "fullness." A rare biblical word.

Mili From Hebrew. A new word coined from the words *mi* "who" and *li* "me," meaning "who is for me?"

Milca From Hebrew, meaning "queen." In the Bible, she is Abraham's niece. Variant spelling: *Milka*.

Minha From Hebrew, meaning "gift."

Mindy Nickname of the Dutch and German name *Wilhelmina*. Yiddish variants: *Mindel, Minna*.

Mira Nickname of the Hebrew name Miriam, meaning "sea of sorrow." Yiddish variant: *Mirel*.

Mirtza From Hebrew, meaning "energetic."

Miryam From Hebrew, meaning "sea of sorrow." She was Moses' and Aaron's sister. Variant spelling: *Miriam*. Variant: *Mary*. Yiddish-Russian nickname form: *Mishke*.

Mishbacha From Hebrew, meaning "excellent."

Mishmeret From Hebrew, meaning "watch tower."

Mitala From Hebrew, meaning "a stream."

Mitzpa From Hebrew, meaning "observation post."

Mivtechet From Hebrew, meaning "secured."

Molada From Hebrew, meaning "homeland." Used also for boys.

Molechet From Hebrew, meaning "female ruler."

Mor From Hebrew, meaning "myrrh."

Morag From Hebrew, meaning "threshing board."

Moran From Hebrew, meaning "(female) teacher."

Morasha From Hebrew, meaning "legacy."

Moriel From Hebrew, meaning "God is my teacher."

Morit From Hebrew, meaning "(female) teacher."

Moryat From Hebrew, meaning "bitter."

Moshe'a Feminine form of the Hebrew name Moshe, meaning "salvation." Variant: *Mosheet*.

Musheet From Hebrew, meaning "feeling."

N

Na'a From Hebrew, meaning "beautiful." Variant: *Nava*.

Na'ama From Hebrew, meaning "pleasant, pretty" or "maiden, young girl." Variants: *Na'amana, Na'ami, Na'amiya*.

Na'amit From Hebrew, designating an ostrich-like bird.

Nacha From Hebrew, meaning "restfulness." Variant: *Nachat*.

Nachmaniya Feminine form of the Hebrew name Nachman, meaning "comfort." Nickname: *Nachmi*.

Nadan From Hebrew, meaning "dowry." Something due by law.

Nafshiya From Hebrew, meaning "soul" or "friendship."

Naftala Feminine form of the Hebrew name Naftali, meaning "to wrestle." Variant: *Naftalya*.

Nagida From Hebrew, meaning "noble female person."

Nahara From Aramaic, meaning "light." Variant: *Nehora*.

Naomi From Hebrew, meaning "delightful" or "beautiful." In the Bible, Ruth's mother-in-law. In Jewish belief, the Messiah will come from Ruth's line. Variant: *Nomi*.

Natanya Feminine form of the Hebrew name Nathan, meaning "God granted."

Nava From Hebrew, meaning "beautiful, pleasing."

Nechama Feminine form of the name Nahum. From Hebrew and Yiddish, meaning "consolation." Yiddish nickname form: *Necha.*

Nedavya From Hebrew, meaning "God's generosity."

Nediva From Hebrew, meaning "generous."

Ne'edra From Hebrew, meaning "glorified." Variant: *Ne'ederet.*

Ne'emana From Hebrew, meaning "faithful, truthful."

Ne'etzala From Hebrew, meaning "perfect."

Negba From Hebrew, meaning "southward."

Ne'ila From Hebrew, meaning "sealing, closing." Final service on Yom Kippur.

Ne'ima From Hebrew, meaning "melody" or "pleasant."

Nera From Hebrew, meaning "candle."

Ne'ira From Hebrew, meaning "The Lord's light."

Nerli From Hebrew, meaning "I have light."

Neshama From Hebrew, meaning "soul." Variant: *Nishmiya*.

Nesia From Hebrew, meaning "God's miracle." Variants: *Nesya, Nessa*.

Nesicha From Hebrew, meaning "princess."

Neta From Hebrew, meaning "shrub" or "plant." Variant: *Netya*.

Netanya From Hebrew, meaning "gift."

Netan'iela From Hebrew, meaning "God's gift." Variant: *Netaniya*.

Neviah From Hebrew, meaning "prophetess."

Nevona From Hebrew, meaning "wise woman."

Nichbada From Hebrew, meaning "respected woman."

Nilbava From Hebrew, meaning "good-natured female." Variant: *Nilbevet*.

Nili A Hebrew acronym taken from the Bible: "The eternity of Israel is not false." Also designating a plant in the pea family. Used also for boys.

Nina From Hebrew, meaning "great-granddaughter." Also a French and Russian nickname form of *Anne*.

Nira From Hebrew, meaning "uncultivated field."

Nirit The Israeli name for a plant with yellow blossoms.

Nirtza From Hebrew, meaning "desirable."

Nissa From Hebrew, meaning "to test."

Nitza From Hebrew, meaning "flower bud." Variant: *Nitzana*.

Nitzchona From Hebrew, meaning "victory."

Niva From Hebrew, meaning "speech."

Nivchora From Hebrew, meaning "chosen."

Noa From Hebrew. In the Bible, a daughter of Zelophehad.

No'adah From Hebrew, meaning "appointed" or "prepared."

No'adya From Hebrew, meaning "appointed by God." A biblical prophetess.

No'am From Hebrew, meaning "sweet, pleasant." Primarily a boys' name.

No'aza From Hebrew, meaning "audacious."

Nodehl'yah From Hebrew, meaning "let us thank God."

Nofiyah From Hebrew, meaning "God's beautiful panorama."

Noga From Hebrew, meaning "bright." One of King David's sons.

Nogah From Hebrew, meaning "morning light."

No'it From Hebrew, meaning "a plant."

Noteret From Hebrew, meaning "protector."

Noya From Hebrew, meaning "ornamented" or "beautiful."

Nufar From Hebrew, meaning "waterlily."

Nura From Aramaic, meaning "light."

Nureen Possibly from Hebrew, meaning "light."

Nurit Israeli name for a plant with red and yellow blossoms.

Nuriya From Aramaic, meaning "God's light."

Oda From Hebrew, meaning "song."

Odeda From Hebrew, meaning "courageous."

Odedya From Hebrew, meaning "I will praise God."

Odera From Hebrew, meaning "plough."

Odiya From Hebrew, meaning "song of God."

Ofira From Hebrew, meaning "golden." In the Bible, there are frequent references to the gold of Ofir. Variant spelling: *Ophira*.

Ofna From Aramaic, meaning "style."

Ofnat From Hebrew, meaning "wheel."

Ofra From Hebrew, meaning "young mountain goat." Also used for boys.

Oganya From Hebrew, meaning "anchor" or "binding."

Ohad From Hebrew, meaning "love, empathy."

Ohela From Hebrew, meaning "tent" or "protection."

Oholiav From Hebrew, meaning "God is my protection." An associate of Bezalel, mentioned in the Bible.

Ola From Hebrew, meaning "female immigrant (to Israel)."

Omrit From Hebrew, meaning "bundle of harvested wheat."

Or From Hebrew, meaning "light." Variants: *Ora, Orit*.

Oralee From Hebrew, meaning "I have light" or "my light."

Orna From Hebrew, meaning "let there be light" or "pine tree." Variants: *Ornit, Ornina*.

Orpah From Hebrew, meaning "to flee" (literally: "to turn one's back"). A Moabite who, unlike Ruth in the biblical story, did not convert to Judaism.

Otzara From Hebrew, meaning "treasure."

Ozera From Hebrew, meaning "helper."

Paz From Hebrew, meaning "gold, golden." Variant: *Pazit*.

Pazya From Hebrew, meaning "God's gold."

Peduya From Hebrew, meaning "redeemed."

Peliah From Hebrew, meaning "miracle, wonder." Variant: *Pili*.

Peninah From Hebrew, meaning "pearl." Elkanah's wife in the Bible.

Perach From Hebrew, meaning "flower" or "blossom."

Peri From Hebrew, meaning "fruit." Also used for boys. Variant spelling: *Perri*.

Peshe From Yiddish, nickname form of Bat-Sheba. Variant: *Pessel*.

Pe'uta From Hebrew, meaning "very tiny."

Pita From Aramaic and Hebrew, meaning "bread."

Pora From Hebrew, meaning "fruitful." Variant: *Poriya*.

Puah From Hebrew, meaning "to cry out." In the Bible, it means "midwife."

R

Raanana From Hebrew, meaning "fresh, luscious."

Rachel From Hebrew, meaning "ewe," symbolizing gentleness. Jacob's favorite wife. Variants: *Rachela*, *Racquel*, *Rochelle*.

Rafya From Hebrew, meaning "God's healing."

Raina From Yiddish, meaning "ruler" or "queen." Variant spelling: *Rayna*.

Raisa From Yiddish, meaning "rose." Variants: *Raize*, *Raizel*.

Rama From Hebrew, meaning "precious, ruby-colored stone" (literally: "lofty"), mentioned in the Bible.

Ramziya From Hebrew, meaning "signal." Nickname: *Rimzi*.

Rani From Hebrew, meaning "my song."

Ranya From Hebrew, meaning "God's song."

Raviva From Hebrew, meaning "raindrop."

Raya From Hebrew, meaning "friend."

Raziela From Hebrew, meaning "God is my secret."

Rafaela Feminine form of the Hebrew name Rafael, meaning "God has healed." In Jewish tradition, Rafael is one of the angels ministering to God.

Rebecca English form of the Hebrew name *Rivka*, possibly meaning "knotted cord." In the Bible, she is Isaac's wife and the mother of Jacob and Esau. Nicknames: *Becky, Riki.*

Refu'a From Hebrew, meaning "healing." Variant: *Rofi.*

Remazya From Hebrew, meaning "sign from God."

Re'uma From Aramaic, meaning "antelope." In the Bible, the concubine of Nahor, Abraham's brother.

Reuvena Feminine form of the Hebrew name Reuven, literally meaning "look — a son!" Reuven was one of Jacob's twelve sons.

Rikma From Hebrew, meaning "woven."

Rikuda From Hebrew, meaning "to dance" or "to prance."

Rimon From Hebrew, meaning "pomegranate." Also used for boys. Variant: *Rimona*.

Rina From Hebrew, meaning "joy." Variant: *Rinat*.

Rinatya From Hebrew, meaning "song of the Lord."

Rishona From Hebrew, meaning "first."

Rishpa From Hebrew, meaning "spark." Variant: *Rishpona*.

Ritzpa From Hebrew, meaning "floor." In the Bible, the daughter of Aya, one of King Saul's concubines.

Ro'ah From Hebrew, meaning "(female) seer."

Romema From Hebrew, meaning "lofty heights." Variants: *Romemit, Romemiya, Romiya*.

Rona From Hebrew, meaning "song." Variant spelling: *Rhona*. Variant: *Ronena*.

Roni From Hebrew, meaning "my song."

Roniya From Hebrew, "God's joy."

Rotem From Hebrew, meaning "to bind." Listed in the Bible, this is a plant that grows in the Negev area in Israel.

Ruchama From Hebrew, meaning "compassion." Variant spelling: *Ruhama*.

Ruth From Hebrew, meaning "friendship." Famous in the Bible as the Moabite daugther-in-law of Naomi, who converts to Judaism and becomes the great-grandmother of King David.

Sa'ada From Hebrew, meaning "support, help." Akin to the male name Sa'adya.

Saba From Hebrew and Aramaic, meaning "aged." In modern Hebrew, it means "grandpa." Also a boy's name.

Sabra From Hebrew, meaning "native-born Israeli" (literally: "prickly pear"). Rationale: tough outside, soft and sweet within.

Salit From Hebrew. Name of a bird indigenous to the south of Israel.

Samantha Name of uncertain origin. Perhaps a feminine version of Samuel.

Samuela Feminine form of the Hebrew name Samuel, meaning "His name is God" or "God heard." In Hebrew: *Shmu'ela*.

Saphira From Hebrew, meaning "sapphire." Variants: *Sapir, Sapirit*.

Sarah From Hebrew, meaning "princess" or "noblewoman." The first biblical matriarch, wife of Abraham and mother of Isaac. Variant spelling: *Sarah, Zara*. Variants: *Sarit*. Nicknames: *Sadie, Sally*. Yiddish nickname forms: *Sura, Sorke, Sorale, Tzirel*.

Sasgona From Aramaic, meaning "multi-colored."

Sasona From Hebrew, meaning "joy."

Savta From Aramaic, meaning "aged." In modern Hebrew, it means "grandma."

Savion From Hebrew, designating a plant of the senecio family.

Segula From Hebrew, meaning "special" or "treasure."

Sela From Hebrew, meaning "a rock." Also a boy's name.

Selila From Hebrew, meaning "path."

Semadar From Hebrew, meaning "bud, blossom." Variant: *Smadar*.

Semaicha From Hebrew, meaning "happy."

Senunit From Hebrew, meaning "bird that is both swift and sweet-singing."

Serach From Hebrew, meaning "to be free." In the Bible, a daughter of Asher. Variant spelling: *Serah*.

Seraphina From Hebrew, meaning "to burn." Akin to the biblical seraphim, the winged angels surrounding God's throne.

Setav From Hebrew, meaning "autumn." Also used for boys.

Sevira From Hebrew, meaning "reasonable."

Seya From Hebrew, meaning "lamb."

Sha'anana From Hebrew, meaning "tranquil."

Shachar From Hebrew, meaning "dawn." Used also for boys.

Shalgit From Hebrew, meaning "snow."

Shalva From Hebrew, meaning "peace."

Shamira From Hebrew, meaning "protector."

Sharon From Hebrew, meaning "flat area, plain." In Israel and in the Bible, it is the south of Mt. Carmel to Jaffa. Variants: *Sharona*, *Sharonit*, *Sharella*.

Shaula Feminine form of the Hebrew name Shaul (English: Saul), meaning "he asked" or "he borrowed."

Shechina From Hebrew, meaning "God's Holy Spirit."

She'era From Hebrew, meaning "survivor" or "remnant." Ephraim's daughter in the Bible.

She'ifa From Hebrew, meaning "yearning."

Sheina From Yiddish, meaning: "beautiful." Variant spelling: *Shaina, Shayna*. Variants: *Shaindel, Shona*.

Shekeda From Hebrew, meaning "almond tree." Variant: *Shekediya*.

Sheli From Hebrew, meaning "mine, belonging to me." Variant spelling: *Shelli*.

Sheliya From Hebrew, meaning "God is mine."

Shetila From Hebrew, meaning "plant."

Sheviviya From Hebrew, meaning "spark of God."

Shifra From Hebrew, meaning "handsome, good." In the Bible, the name of a midwife who helped deliver Moses.

Shikma From Hebrew, meaning "sycamore tree." Variant: *Shikmona*.

Shimona Feminine form of the Hebrew name Shimon (English: Simon), meaning "to hear" or "to be heard."

Shimshona Feminine form of the name Shimshon (English: Samson), meaning "sun."

Shira From Hebrew, meaning "song" or "poem."

Shir'el From Hebrew, meaning "God's song."

Shita From Hebrew, meaning "acacia tree."

Shlomit From Hebrew, meaning "peaceful." Akin to *Shulamit.*

Shmuela Feminine Hebrew form of the name Samuel, meaning "His name is God" or "God heard."

Shoshana From Hebrew, a synonym for a rose or a lily. In the Midrash it is a generic term for a flower. English equivalent: *Susan.*

Shprintza A Yiddish form of the Spanish name *Esperanza*, meaning "hope." Nickname: *Shprintzel.*

Shu'a From Aramaic, meaning "salvation."

Shuala From Hebrew, meaning "(female) fox."

Shulamit From Hebrew, meaning "peaceful." In the Bible, the Shunamite woman, the most beautiful in all Israel, is believed to be named Shulamit.

Shura From Hebrew, meaning "a line."

Sigal From Hebrew, meaning "treasure."

Silona From Hebrew and Greek, meaning "a stream."

Sima From Aramaic, meaning "treasure."

Simcha From Hebrew, meaning "joy" or "joyous event." Used also for boys. Variants: *Simchona, Simchit.*

Siona From Hebrew, meaning "Zion" (literally: "superb"). *Tziyona* in Hebrew.

Sisel From Yiddish, meaning "sweet." Variant spelling: *Zisel.*

Sisi From Hebrew, meaning "my joy." Related to the English name *Cecilia.*

Sivana Feminine form of the Hebrew month Sivan, the Hebrew month usually falling in May or June.

Tachan From Hebrew, meaning "to pray" or "petition."

Tafat From Hebrew, meaning "to trickle." One of King Solomon's daughters.

Tal From Hebrew, meaning "dew." Nickname: *Tali.*

Talia From Aramaic, meaning "young lamb."

Talila From Hebrew, meaning "covering of dew." Variants: *Talal*, *Talora*.

Tamah From Hebrew, meaning "surprise, wonder" or "whole."

Tamar From Hebrew, meaning "palm tree" or "upright." Variant: *Tamara*.

Tavora From Hebrew. Variant form of biblical Mt. Tabor.

Techiya From Hebrew, meaning "rebirth."

Tehila From Hebrew, meaning "praise, song of praise."

Teriya From Hebrew, meaning "ripe" or "fresh." Variant spelling: *Tari*, *Teria*.

Terufa From Hebrew, meaning "healing."

Teruma From Hebrew, meaning "offering" or "gift."

Tifara From Hebrew, meaning "glory" or "beautiful."

Tikva From Hebrew, meaning "hope." Used also for boys.

Tirtza From Hebrew, meaning "pleasing" or "willing." In the Bible, a daughter of Zelophachad.

Tova From Hebrew, meaning "good." Yiddish variant: *Gittel*. Usual English equivalent: *Bonnie*.

Tzadika From Hebrew, meaning "pious woman."

Tzedaka From Hebrew, meaning "charity."

Tz'huva From Hebrew, meaning "golden."

Tze'ira From Hebrew, meaning "young girl."

Tzeviah From Hebrew, meaning "gazelle" or "deer." In the Bible, she is King Yehoash's mother.

𝕌

Uma From Hebrew, meaning "nation."

Uriela From Hebrew, meaning "God's delight."

Ushriya From Hebrew, meaning "blessed of God."

Uziela From Hebrew, meaning "my strength is the Lord."

𝕍

Varda From Hebrew, meaning "rose." Variants: *Vardina*, *Vered*.

Velvela Feminine form of the Yiddish nickname Velvel, meaning "wolf."

Ỹ

Ya'el From Hebrew, meaning "to ascend." In the Bible, a Kenite woman in the time of Deborah who killed the enemy general, Sisera.

Ya'en From Hebrew, meaning "ostrich."

Yaffa From Hebrew, meaning "beautiful."

Yahaloma From Hebrew, meaning "precious stone, diamond." Mentioned in the Bible.

Yahel From Hebrew, meaning "to shine."

Ya'ira Feminine form of the Hebrew name Ya'ir, meaning "to bring light."

Yama From Hebrew, meaning "westward" (literally: "toward the sea").

Yamit From Hebrew, meaning "maritime, connected to the sea." Literally, westward.

Yardena Feminine form of the Hebrew name Yarden, meaning "flowing down." Equivalent to English: *Jordana*.

Yardeniya From Hebrew, meaning "garden of the Lord."

Yarona From Hebrew, meaning "to sing."

Yavne'ela From Hebrew, meaning "God builds."

Yechiela Feminine form of the Hebrew name Yechiel, meaning "may God live."

Yedida From Hebrew, meaning "female friend" or "beloved."

Yedidya From Hebrew, "beloved by God" or "friend of God."

Yehosheva From Hebrew, meaning "God's oath." In the Bible, a daughter of King Yoram of Judah.

Yehudit From Hebrew, literally meaning "Jewess." English form: *Judith*.

Yemina From Hebrew, meaning "right hand," signifying strength.

Yenta From Yiddish, meaning "busybody." The origin is not clear: it may come from the Spanish name *Juanita*, the French *Gentille*, or the English *Henrietta*.

Ye'ora From Hebrew, meaning "light."

Yeruchama From Hebrew, meaning "compassion."

Yerusha From Hebrew, meaning "inheritance." In the Bible, she is King Uziah's wife.

Yeshara From Hebrew, meaning "honest" or "straight-forward."

Yeshu'ah From Hebrew, meaning "salvation."

Yif'ah From Hebrew, meaning "splendor."

Yisraela From Hebrew, a variant of *Yisraelit*, meaning "female Israeli"

Yizre'ela From Hebrew, meaning "God will plant."

Yocheved From Hebrew, meaning "God's glory." The name of Moses' mother.

Yona From Hebrew, meaning "dove." Also a boy's name. Variants: *Yonat, Yonina, Yonit.*

Yovela From Hebrew, meaning "jubilee" or "rejoicing."

Yutke From Yiddish, a nickname form of *Yehudit* (English: *Judith*).

Z

Zahara From Hebrew, meaning "shining."

Zehava From Hebrew, meaning "golden."

Zemira From Hebrew, meaning "melody."

Zemora From Hebrew, meaning "branch."

Zipora From Hebrew, meaning "bird."

Ziva From Hebrew, meaning "brightness."

Zlata A Yiddish name related to the name *Golda*. Popular name in Poland.

Boys' Names

𝕬

Aaron From Hebrew, possibly meaning "high mountain." Moses' brother and the first High Priest in Jewish history. Variant spelling: *Aron*. Nickname: *Arele*.

Abaye From Aramaic, meaning "little father."

Abba From Hebrew and Aramaic, meaning "father." Nickname: *Abbale*.

Abir From Hebrew, meaning "strong."

Abner From Hebrew, meaning "father of light." In the Bible, King Saul's general. Hebrew form: *Avner*. Nickname: *Abbie*.

Abraham From Hebrew, meaning "father of a vast people." Considered the first Jew and the first biblical patriarch. Nickname: *Abe*.

Absalom From Hebrew, meaning "father of peace." King David's third son. Variant: *Avshalom*.

Achai From Aramaic, meaning "my brother."

Achazia From Hebrew, meaning "God has grasped."

Achban From Hebrew, meaning "brother of a sage."

Achi From Hebrew, meaning "my brother." A leader of Gad's tribe in the Bible.

Achi'av From Hebrew, meaning "father's brother."

Achiezer From Hebrew, meaning "my brother is my helper."

Achiman From Hebrew, meaning "my brother is a gift."

Achimelech From Hebrew, meaning "the king (God) is my brother."

Achinadav From Aramaic, meaning "my brother is noble." A famous talmudic scholar.

Achiner From Hebrew, meaning "my brother is light."

Achinoam From Hebrew, meaning "my brother is a delight."

Achisar From Hebrew, meaning "my brother is a prince."

Achishachar From Hebrew, meaning "my brother is the dawn." In the Bible, a member of the tribe of Benjamin.

Adam From Hebrew, meaning "man of the earth." First man or human being mentioned in the Bible.

Adiel From Hebrew, meaning "God is my adornment." Nickname: *Adi.*

Adin From Hebrew, meaning "pleasant, beautiful."

Adlai From Aramaic, meaning "God's refuge."

Adriel From Hebrew, meaning "God is my master."

Akiva From Hebrew, related to the name *Yaacov* (English: *Jacob*). Rabbi Akiva is considered one of the greatest Jewish scholars of all time.

Alef From Hebrew, meaning "chief" or "number one." It is also the first letter of the Hebrew alphabet.

Alon From Hebrew, meaning "oak tree."

Alter From Yiddish, meaning "old one." Centuries ago, male babies were often given this name in the hope that they would live long.

Ami From Hebrew, meaning "my people."

Amichai From Hebrew, meaning "my people lives."

Amidror From Hebrew, meaning " my people is free."

Amiel From Hebrew, meaning "God of my people."

Amit From Hebrew, meaning "friend."

Amitai From Hebrew, meaning "truth." In the Bible, he was Jonah's father.

Amnon From Hebrew, meaning "faithful." King David's eldest son.

Amos From Hebrew, meaning "one who is burdened." A prominent prophet in the Bible.

Amotz From Hebrew, meaning "courageous."

Amram From Hebrew, meaning "mighty nation." Moses' father in the Bible.

Anshel From Yiddish, a popular form of the name *Asher*.

Ardon From Hebrew, meaning "bronze." Mentioned in the Bible, he was Caleb's son.

Ari From Hebrew, meaning "lion," connoting strength. Akin to *Aryeh*.

Ariel From Hebrew, meaning "lion of God." Variant spelling: *Arel*. Nickname: *Arik*.

Armon From Hebrew, meaning "palace." A son of King Saul.

Arnon From Hebrew, meaning "strong stream." In the Bible, it flows into the Dead Sea.

Asa From Hebrew, meaning "healer." He was a king of Judah.

Asaf From Hebrew, meaning "one who is a gatherer."

Asiel From Hebrew, meaning "God has created." In the Bible, a brother of Joab.

Asher From Hebrew, meaning "fortunate, blessed." One of Jacob's twelve sons.

Atid From Hebrew, meaning "the future."

Atir From Hebrew, meaning "crown" or "ornament."

Avi From Hebrew, meaning "my father."

Aviam From Hebrew, meaning "father of the nation."

Aviav From Hebrew, meaning "grandfather."

Avichai From Hebrew, meaning "father lives on."

Avidan From Hebrew, "God is just."

Avidor From Hebrew, meaning "father of a generation."

Aviel From Hebrew, meaning "God is my father."

Aviezer From Hebrew, meaning "my father is salvation."

Avigdor From Hebrew, meaning "father the protector."

Avimelech From Hebrew, meaning "my father is king."

Avinoam From Hebrew, meaning "father of delight."

Avital From Hebrew, meaning "father of dew." Used also for girls.

Aviv From Hebrew, meaning "spring" or "youthful."

Avniel From Hebrew, meaning "God is my strength."

Avinadav From Hebrew, meaning "my father is noble."

Avinatan From Hebrew, meaning "my father has given."

Avishai From Hebrew, meaning "father's gift."

Avituv From Hebrew, meaning "father of goodness."

Ayal From Hebrew, meaning "a ram." Variant spelling: *Eyal*.

Azariah From Hebrew, meaning "the help of God."

Aziz From Hebrew, meaning "strength."

Azriel From Hebrew, meaning "God is my help."

B

Bachya From Aramaic, meaning "life."

Bahir From Hebrew, meaning "bright."

Balfour A recently-coined name honoring the British statesman whose efforts helped bring about the establishment of Israel.

Barak From Hebrew, meaning "lightning."

Baran From Aramaic, meaning "son of the people."

Bar-Ilan From Aramaic, meaning "fruit of a tree."

Bar-Kochba From Aramaic, meaning "son of a star." A military leader thought by some to be the Messiah.

Baruch From Hebrew, meaning "blessed."

Barzilai From Aramaic, meaning "man of iron."

Bava From Aramaic, meaning "gate." A famous talmudic scholar.

Bazak From Hebrew, meaning "flash of light."

Ben From Hebrew, meaning "son."

Ben-Ad From Hebrew, meaning "eternal."

Ben-Ami From Hebrew, meaning "son of my people."

Ben-Azai From Aramaic and Hebrew, meaning "son of strength."

Ben-Chayil From Hebrew, meaning "son of courage."

Ben-Chen From Hebrew, meaning "son of graciousness."

Ben-Chesed From Hebrew, meaning "merciful person."

Ben-Ezra From Hebrew, meaning "son of salvation."

Benjamin Anglicized version of *Binyamin*, one of Jacob's twelve sons. Originally from Hebrew, meaning "son of my right hand." Nickname: *Ben*, *Benny* (English form), *Bibi* (Israeli form).

Benor From Hebrew, meaning "son of light."

Ben Tov From Hebrew, meaning "good son."

Benzion From Hebrew, meaning "son of Zion," signifying excellence. Hebrew spelling: *Ben-Tziyon*. Nickname: *Bentzi*.

Ber From Yiddish, meaning "bear." Hebrew equivalent: *Dov*.

Beryl From Yiddish, diminutive of *Ber*.

Bezalel From Hebrew, meaning "shadow of God," in other words: God will protect. In the Bible Bezalel was a master artisan. Variant spelling: *Betzalel*.

Bilgah From Hebrew, meaning "cheer, joyousness."

Boaz From Hebrew, meaning "strength." The husband of Ruth in the Bible, after she was widowed.

Buki From Hebrew, meaning "tested" or "bottle."

Buna From Hebrew, meaning "knowledge, understanding."

Bustan From Persian, meaning "garden."

Carmel From Hebrew, meaning "God's vineyard." Variant: *Carmiel*. Nickname: *Carmi*.

Catriel From Hebrew, meaning "crown of God."

Chag From Hebrew, meaning "holiday."

Chagai From Aramaic and Hebrew, meaning "my festivals."

Chagiga From Hebrew, meaning "festival of God."

Chaim From Hebrew, meaning "life." English equivalent: *Vivien*. Variant spelling: *Hayyim*. Variant: *Chai*. Nickname: *Hy*.

Chalil From Hebrew, meaning "flute."

Chamud From Hebrew, meaning "precious" or "loved one."

Chamu'el From Hebrew, meaning "saved by God."

Chananya From Hebrew, meaning "God's compassion."

Chanina From Aramaic, meaning "gracious." Variant:
Chanan.

Chanoch From Hebrew, meaning "educated" or
"consecrated."

Chasdiel From Hebrew, meaning "my God is gracious."

Chasid From Hebrew, meaning "righteous" or "pious
person."

Chasiel From Hebrew, meaning "God's refuge."

Chatzkel From Yiddish, a nickname for *Ezekiel*, meaning
"God will strengthen."

Chavakuk From Hebrew. One of the minor prophets,
included in the Bible. Variant spelling: *Havakuk.*

Chaviv From Hebrew, meaning "beloved."

Chaziel From Hebrew, meaning "vision of God."

Chemdad From Hebrew, meaning "beloved" or
"precious." Variant: *Chemdan.*

Chen From Hebrew, meaning "charm."

Chermon From Hebrew, meaning "sacred." Variant spelling: *Hermon*.

Cherut From Hebrew, meaning "liberty." Variant spelling: *Herut*.

Cheshvan From Hebrew, a month in the Jewish calendar. Variant spelling: *Heshvan*.

Chiya From Hebrew, nickname of *Yechiel*, meaning "may God live."

Chizkiya From Hebrew, meaning "God is my strength."

Choni From Hebrew, meaning "gracious." Variant spelling: *Honi*.

Chovev From Hebrew, meaning "friend" or "lover."

Cobie A nickname for *Yaacov* (English: *Jacob*), meaning "held by the heel."

Coresh The Hebrew name of *Cyrus*, the king of ancient Persia, who allowed the Jewish captives—after the destruction of the first Holy Temple—to return home.

Dagan From Hebrew, meaning "grain" or "corn."

Dagul From Hebrew, meaning "emblem."

Dan From Hebrew, meaning "he judged." One of Jacob's twelve sons; hence, founder of one of the Twelve Tribes. Nickname: *Dani.*

Daniel From Hebrew, meaning "God is my judge." Famous biblical figure, who escaped from the lion's den.

Dar From Hebrew, meaning "pearl."

David From Hebrew, meaning "beloved." Israel's greatest king, a towering biblical figure. In postbiblical centuries, no talmudic rabbi ever had that name. Today it is universally popular. Nickname forms: *Dave, Davy.* In Yiddish: *Dovidel.*

Datiel From Hebrew, meaning "knowledge of God."

Dayan From Hebrew, meaning "a judge." Used also for girls.

Dekel From Arabic, meaning "palm or date tree."

Deror From Hebrew, meaning "freedom" or "a swallow." Variant: *D'ror.*

Devir From Hebrew, meaning "the holiest room (in the Temple)."

Dishon From Hebrew, meaning "threshing." Mentioned in the Bible.

Divri From Hebrew, meaning "orator." Variant: *Dibri*.

Dodo From Hebrew, meaning "beloved." A member of the tribe of Issachar.

Dor From Hebrew, meaning "generation."

Doron From Hebrew, meaning "gift."

Dotan From Hebrew, meaning "law," Also an ancient Israeli place name. Variant spelling: *Dothan*.

Dov From Hebrew, meaning "bear."

Dovev From Hebrew, meaning "to whisper" or "to speak."

Dubi From Hebrew, meaning "my bear."

Dur From Hebrew, meaning "to encircle" or "to pile up."

Duriel From Hebrew, meaning "God is my dwelling place."

Echud From Hebrew, meaning "unity." Variant spelling: *Ehud*.

Eden From Hebrew, meaning "paradise." First home of Adam and Eve.

Efer From Hebrew, meaning "young mountain goat."

Efrat From Hebrew, meaning "distinguished." A member of Ephraim's tribe. Also used for girls.

Efraim From Hebrew, meaning "fruitful." One of Joseph's sons. Variant spelling: *Ephraim*.

Efron From Hebrew, meaning "bird." In the Bible, a man who sold a burial plot to Abraham.

Ehud From Hebrew, meaning "love." Also name of a judge mentioned in the Bible. Nickname: *Udi*.

Eidi From Hebrew, meaning "my witness."

Eilon From Hebrew, meaning "oak tree." In the Bible, a grandson of Jacob. Also name of a judge from the Zebulun tribe.

Eitan From Hebrew, meaning "strong."

Eizer From Hebrew, name of an officer mentioned in the Bible. In Yiddish, nickname form for *Eliezer*. Variant: *Ezer*.

Elad From Hebrew, meaning "God is eternal."

Elami From Hebrew, meaning "to my people."

Elazar From Hebrew, meaning "God has helped." Son of Aaron, the High Priest. Popular name among talmudic scholars.

Eldar From Hebrew, meaning "where God lives."

Elez From Hebrew, meaning "joy."

Eli From Hebrew, meaning "my God." Also meaning "ascent" or "lifting upwards." The last of the judges in the Bible. Variant: *Eliahu*.

Eliav From Hebrew, meaning "my God is father."

Eliezer From Hebrew, meaning "his God has helped." Abraham's trusted servant.

Elihu From Hebrew, meaning "he is my God." Nickname: *Lihu*.

Elijah From Hebrew, meaning "the Lord is my God." One of the earliest Hebrew prophets. Jewish tradition says he will announce the advent of the Messiah. Hebrew form: *Eliyahu*.

Elimelech From Hebrew, meaning "my God is king."

Elisha From Hebrew, meaning "God is my salvation." He was Elijah's successor.

Elkan From Hebrew, meaning "God has purchased." Original Hebrew form: *Elkana*.

Elul From Hebrew, a month in the Jewish calendar.

Elrad From Hebrew, meaning "God is the ruler."

Emanuel From Hebrew, meaning "God is with us," connoting divine support.

Emmet From Hebrew, meaning "truth." Variant spelling: *Emet*.

Enoch From Hebrew, meaning "educated." Enoch was a son born to Adam and Eve after Cain killed Abel.

Eshkol From Hebrew, meaning "cluster of grapes." Among Jewish scholars, the name signifies great respectfulness.

Etan From Hebrew, meaning "strong." Variant spellings: *Ethan, Eitan*.

Ezekiel From Hebrew, meaning "God will strengthen." One of three major biblical prophets.

Ezra From Hebrew, meaning "help." Variants: *Azariah, Ezer*.

Feibel Yiddish adaptation of the Greek name *Phoebus*. Variant: *Feibush*.

Fishel From Yiddish, meaning "a fish" or "to be fruitful like a fish." Some believe it is related to the Hebrew name *Ephraim*. Nickname: Fishke.

Gabriel From Hebrew, meaning "God is my strength." One of the four angels said to be ministering to God. Daniel, in the Bible, sees the angel Gabriel in a vision. Nicknames: *Gabe, Gabie, Gabby*.

Gad From Hebrew, meaning "happy" or "warrior." One of Jacob's twelve sons.

Gadi From Arabic, meaning "my fortune."

Gadiel From Hebrew, meaning "God is my blessing." A member of Zebulun tribe.

Gafni From Hebrew, meaning "my vineyard."

Galya From Hebrew, meaning "the Lord's hill."

Gamaliel From Hebrew, meaning "God is my reward," connoting a blessing. Variant: *Gamliel*.

Ge'alya From Hebrew, meaning "God redeems."

Gedaliah From Hebrew, meaning "God is great." In the Bible, he was a governor of Judea, under the Babylonians.

Gefanya From Hebrew, meaning "vineyard of the Lord."

Gefen From Hebrew, meaning "a vine."

Gemali From Hebrew, meaning "my reward."

Gershom From Hebrew, meaning "stranger." In the Bible, Gershom was Moses' son. Variants: *Gershon, Gerson*.

Ge'uel From Hebrew, meaning "God's majesty."

Geva From Hebrew, meaning "hill." A biblical place name.

Gevarya From Hebrew, meaning "God's might."

Gibor From Hebrew, meaning "strong" or "hero."

Gideon From Hebrew, meaning "great warrior." In the Bible, Gideon is a great warrior-hero who helped conquer the Holy Land. He was also a famous judge who defeated the Midianites. Variant spelling: *Gidon*. Nickname: *Gidi*.

Gil From Hebrew, meaning "joy." *Gili* means "my joy." Used also for girls.

Gilad From Arabic, meaning "a camel's hump," indicating height. Also the name of a mountain range east of the Jordan river. Variant: *Gilead*.

Gilalai From Hebrew, meaning "to roll away." In the Bible, a musician during the time of Ezra.

Gilam From Hebrew, meaning "the people's joy."

Ginton From Hebrew, meaning "orchard, garden." In the Bible, a priest who returned to Jerusalem from Babylonian captivity.

Giora From Aramaic, meaning "stranger" or "convert" (to Judaism).

Gitai From Hebrew, meaning "someone who presses grapes." Variant: *Giti*.

Givol From Hebrew, meaning "in bloom."

Givon From Hebrew, a biblical place name indicating a hill.

Go'el From Hebrew, meaning "the redeemer."

Golan From Hebrew, meaning "a refuge."

Gomer From Hebrew, meaning "to complete, to finish."

Gonen From Hebrew, meaning "protector."

Gur From Hebrew, meaning "a young lion cub."

Guriel From Hebrew, meaning "God is my lion."

Gurion From Hebrew, meaning "strength" or "lion."

H

Hadar From Hebrew, meaning "glory." Used also for girls.

Hadriel From Hebrew, meaning "God's glory."

Hanan From Hebrew, a shortened version of *Yochanan*, meaning "graciousness."

Haran From Hebrew, meaning "mountaineer." Abraham's brother in the Bible.

Harel From Hebrew, meaning "God's mountain." A place name in the Bible.

Haskel From Yiddish, a diminutive form of the prophet's name, *Ezekiel*. A modern Hebrew translation means "wisdom, understanding."

Havakuk From Hebrew, meaning "to embrace." A minor prophet in the Bible.

Helem From Hebrew, meaning "a hammer" or "to strike down." In the Bible, a member of Asher's tribe.

Heman From Hebrew, meaning "faithful." The name appears several times in the Bible.

Hersh From Yiddish, meaning "deer," connoting speed. Hebrew equivalent: *Zvi.* Usual English corresponding names: *Harry, Harold, Henry.* Variant spelling: Hirsh. Nickname form: *Hertzel.*

Herzl Name to memorialize Theodor Herzl, the founder of the Zionist movement.

Hillel From Hebrew, meaning "the shining one" or "praised." One of the greatest Jewish scholars who interpreted Jewish law gently and compassionately.

Hiram From Hebrew, meaning "exalted" or "noble-born brother."

Hod From Hebrew, meaning "splendor" or "vigor."

Hodiya From Hebrew, "praise the Lord" or "God is my splendor." Used also for girls.

Honi From Hebrew, meaning "gracious." Related to the girls' name Hannah.

Hoshaya From Hebrew, meaning "God is salvation." A famous Talmudic scholar.

Huna From Aramaic, meaning "wealth." Talmudic scholar during Babylonian era.

I

Ila From Aramaic, meaning "lofty, exalted."

Ilai From Hebrew, meaning "superior." One of King David's warriors.

Ilan From Hebrew, meaning "tree."

Imishai From Hebrew, meaning "my mother's gift."

Isaac From Hebrew, meaning "he will laugh." One of the three forefathers of the Jewish people. Hebrew equivalent: *Yitzchak*. Popular Yiddish variant: *Itzik*. Nicknames: *Zak*, *Zaki* (Hebrew), *Ike* (English).

Isaiah From Hebrew, meaning "God is salvation." One of the greatest biblical prophets, he lived in the eighth century before B.C.

Ish-Sechel From Hebrew, meaning "man of wisdom."

Ish-Shalom From Hebrew, meaning "man of peace."

Ish-Tov From Hebrew, meaning "good man." In the Bible, King David's foe.

Isser From Yiddish, a nickname form of *Yisra'el* (Israel.)

Isidor From Greek, meaning "gift of Isis." It was a popular name among Jewish immigrants. Nicknames: *Dore*, *Izzy*.

Israel From Hebrew, meaning "prince of God." It is the name given to Jacob after he wrestled with an angel, in the biblical account. The modern translation is "fighter."

Issachar From Hebrew, meaning "there is a reward." One of Jacob's twelve sons.

Itai From Hebrew, meaning "friendly." A great warrior under King David.

Itamar From Hebrew, meaning "island of palm trees."

Itiel From Hebrew, meaning "God is with me." A member of Benjamin's tribe in the Bible.

Ivri From Hebrew, literally meaning "a Hebrew." Abraham was the first to be called a Hebrew; the word nowadays is used mostly for the language.

J

Jacob From Hebrew, meaning "held by the heel," so
named because of the way he was born, holding on
to his brother Esau's heel. Together with his father
Isaac and grandfather Abraham, he is regarded as a
biblical patriarch. His twelve sons were the founders
of the Twelve Tribes of Israel. Hebrew form: *Yaacov*.
Variants: *James, Jacques*. Nicknames: *Yankel*
(Yiddish), *Kobie* (Hebrew).

Japhet From Hebrew, one of Noah's three sons.

Jared From Hebrew. The Bible lists him as Methuselah's
grandfather.

Jaron From Hebrew, meaning "to sing out."

Jedidya From Hebrew, meaning "friend of God." King
Solomon is described by this name. Nickname: *Didi*,
meaning "beloved."

Jeho'ash From Hebrew, meaning "God is strong." A
biblical king of Israel. Variant spelling: *Yeho'ash*. The
translator of the entire Hebrew Bible into Yiddish, in
modern times.

Jehochanan From Hebrew, meaning "God is gracious."
In the era of Ezra the Scribe, he was the High Priest
of Jerusalem. Variant: *Jochanan*.

Jehoram From Hebrew, meaning "God is exalted." A son of king Ahab. Variants: *Joram, Yoram.*

Jehoshafat From Hebrew, meaning "God will judge." A king of Judah.

Jehoyakim From Hebrew, meaning "God will establish." A king of Judah.

Jekutiel From Hebrew, meaning "God will provide." Variant spelling: *Yekutiel.* Nickname: *Kuti.*

Jeremiah From Hebrew, meaning "God will raise up." One of the Bible's chief prophets, descended from a distinguished priestly family. Variant: *Jeremy.*

Jesse From Hebrew, meaning "gift." In the Bible, he is King David's father.

Joab From Hebrew, meaning "God is father." A name usually reserved for a ruler.

Jochanan From Hebrew, meaning "God is gracious." Very popular name during talmudic times.

Joel From Hebrew, meaning "God is willing." A minor prophet included in the Hebrew Bible. Popular Yiddish diminutive: *Yale.*

Jonah From Hebrew, meaning "dove." Famous as the biblical prophet in the belly of a big fish. Greek version: *Jonas.*

Jonathan From Hebrew, meaning "God has given." King Saul's son and David's devoted friend. Nicknames: *Jon*, *Jonny*, *Yoni* (in Israel).

Jordan From Hebrew, meaning "flowing down." Nickname: *Jordie*.

Jose Related to Joseph, pronounced "Yosi." It is regarded today as a Latino name only, but in talmudic times it was widely used by scholars and rabbis.

Joseph From Hebrew, meaning "he will increase." Universally popular name: *Yosef* in Hebrew, *Joe* or *Joey* in English, *Guiseppe* or *Pepo* in Italian, *Yussuf* in Arabic, *Jose* in Spanish, *Josko* in Slavic languages. Yiddish pet name: *Yussel*. Biblical Joseph was one of Jacob's twelve sons.

Joshua From Hebrew, meaning "God is my salvation." Moses' successor who led the Israelites into the Promised Land. Originally his name was Hoshe'a, but Moses added the prefix Yah- for "God." Variant: *Jason*. Nickname: *Josh*.

Josiah From Hebrew, meaning "the Lord's fire." From the age of eight he was king of Judah after his father Amon was murdered.

Jotham From Hebrew, meaning "God is perfect." The youngest of Gideon's seventy sons in the Bible. Variant spelling: *Yotam*.

Judah From Hebrew, meaning "praise." The fourth of Jacob's twelve sons. When the Ten Lost Tribes disappeared into history, only Judah and Benjamin survived, with the former dominant. Nowadays all Jews are descended from Judah, which absorbed Benjamin. The Hebrew word for a Jew is Yehudi, which stems from the Hebrew word for Judah (Yehudah). Variant: *Judd*.

𝕶

Kadmiel From Hebrew, meaning "God is the ancient one." Kadmiel in the Bible is a Levite.

Kadosh From Hebrew, meaning "holy" or "holy person."

Kahana From Aramaic, meaning "priest." A famous talmudic scholar.

Kalil From Hebrew, meaning "wreath." The Talmud lists him as the father of the great scholar Abayeh.

Kalul From Hebrew, meaning "whole" or "perfect."

Kalman A shortened form of the Latin name Kalonymous, meaning "gracious." A 14ᵀᴴ century Jewish scholar named Kalonymous ben Kalonymous translated important texts from Arabic to Hebrew and may have given the mistaken impression that this is a Hebrew name, especially since it bears a Hebraic sound.

Kaniel From Hebrew, meaning "reed," indicating uprightness and strength.

Kapara From Aramaic, meaning "atonement."

Kareem From Arabic, meaning "exalted, noble." Variant spelling: *Karim*.

Karmel From Hebrew, meaning "vineyard of God." Variant spelling: *Carmel*.

Karmi From Hebrew, meaning "my vineyard." Reuben's son in the Bible.

Karmiel From Hebrew, meaning "God is my vineyard." Variant spelling: *Carmiel*.

Karniel From Hebrew, meaning "God is my ray."

Kashti From Hebrew, meaning "my rainbow" or "my bow."

Katriel From Hebrew, meaning "God's crown."

Katzir From Hebrew, meaning "harvest." Boys born on Shavuot, a harvest festival, are often given this name.

Kedar From Hebrew, meaning "swarthy, black." Ishmael's son, mentioned in Genesis.

Kedem From Hebrew, meaning "eastward." Variant: *Kedma.*

Kemu'el From Hebrew, meaning "stand up for God."

Kenanya From Hebrew, meaning "upright, honest." In the Bible, he was in charge of the Temple choir.

Keshet From Hebrew, meaning "rainbow." Boys born on Lag b'Omer are sometimes given this name.

Keskel From Yiddish, a variant of *Yechezkiel*, the Hebrew name of the prophet *Ezekiel.*

Kfir From Hebrew, meaning "young lion." Variant spelling: *Cfir.*

Kish From Hebrew, meaning "a bow." King Saul's father. Variant: *Kishoni.*

Kitron From Hebrew, meaning "a crown."

Kivi From Hebrew, a diminutive of the names *Yaacov* (Jacob) and *Akiva.*

Kobi From Hebrew, a nickname form of *Yaacov* (Jacob).

Kochav From Hebrew, meaning "star." Variant: *Kochva*.

Kolaya From Hebrew, meaning "the voice of God." The prophet Ahab's father.

Komem From Hebrew, meaning "he restored." Akin to the Hebrew word "komemi'yut," which means independence.

Konanya From Hebrew, meaning "God's establishment."

Koren From Hebrew, meaning "shining."

Kotz From Hebrew, meaning "thorn." A leader of the tribe of Judah.

Kushiyahu From Hebrew, meaning "lure of the Lord." A Levite listed in the Bible.

𝕷

Label From Yiddish, nickname for *Leib*, meaning "lion." Variant: *Leibush*.

La'el From Hebrew, meaning "belonging to God."

Lahav From Hebrew, meaning "flame."

Lapid From Hebrew, meaning "torch."

Latif From Hebrew, meaning "affectionate."

Layish From Hebrew, meaning "lion."

Lavi From Hebrew, meaning "lion."

Lazer From Yiddish, a nickname form of *Eliezer*.

Lemel From Yiddish, meaning "little lamb," connoting a meek person.

Lemuel From Hebrew, meaning "belonging to God." An additional name for King Solomon. Nickname: *Lem*.

Leon From Greek and Latin, meaning "lion." Many Jews bear this name mistaking it for a Jewish name. Variants: *Leo*, *Leonard*. Yiddish equivalent: *Leib*.

Le'or From Hebrew, meaning "to the light."

Leshem From Hebrew, meaning "precious stone" or "amber" that the High Priest wore in his breastplate during Temple days.

Lesser From Yiddish, a variant of the Yiddish nickname, *Lazer*.

Lev From Hebrew, meaning "heart."

Levi From Hebrew, meaning "joined to." Jacob's and Lea's son from whom descended the priests who served in the Holy Temple.

Levana From Hebrew, meaning "moon." Used also for girls.

Levitas From Hebrew, a variant of *Levi*. A 2ND century Palestinian scholar by that name is listed in the Talmud.

Le'umi From Hebrew, meaning "national."

Li'ad From Hebrew, meaning "eternity is mine."

Li'am From Hebrew, meaning "my people."

Li'av From Hebrew, meaning "my father," referring to God.

Lieber From Yiddish, meaning "beloved." The Scandinavian name *Leif* is believed to be a variant of the name. Variant spelling: *Liber*.

Li'hu From Hebrew, meaning "I belong to him." Also a nickname form of *Elihu*.

Likchi From Hebrew, meaning "my teaching." A member of the Menashe tribe had that name.

Li'on From Hebrew, meaning "I have strength." Variants: *Lionel*, *Lyon*.

Li'or From Hebrew, meaning "I have light."

Liron From Hebrew, meaning "I have a song." Variant spelling: *Leron*.

Lital From Hebrew, meaning "I have dew."

Litov From Hebrew, meaning "I have good fortune."

Livne From Hebrew, meaning "poplar tree, used in ancient times in idolatry rites."

Lopez From Spanish, meaning "wolf." Associated with Benjamin, who is likened to a wolf in the Bible. Variants: *Lupo, Lupez.*

Luz From Hebrew, meaning "almond tree."

M

Ma'adai From Aramaic, meaning "delight." Variant: *Ma'adia.*

Ma'arav From Hebrew, meaning "westward."

Ma'ayan From Hebrew, meaning "fountain, spring." Used also for girls.

Ma'aziya From Hebrew, meaning "strength of the Lord."

Maccabee From Hebrew, an acronym meaning "Who is like Thee, O God." It was the battle cry of the Jews against the Greco-Syrian oppressors, which led to the cleansing or rededication of the Holy Temple. This event is celebrated every year by the festival of Chanukah.

Machol From Hebrew, meaning "dance." He is the father of three wise sons, in the biblical account.

Madai From Hebrew, meaning "strife." Noah's grandson, son of Japhet.

Magal From Hebrew, meaning "scythe." Boys and girls born on Shavuot, a harvest festival, are often given this name.

Magen From Hebrew, meaning "shield" or "defender."

Magdiel From Hebrew, meaning "goodness of the Lord."

Maharai From Aramaic, meaning "haste." One of King David's warriors.

Mahir From Hebrew, meaning "industrious, expert."

Mahlon From Hebrew. Ruth's first husband, he was the son of Naomi and Elimelech.

Maimon From Arabic, meaning "good fortune." Regarded as a tribute to the great scholar-rabbi-physician, Maimonides.

Maksim From Hebrew, meaning "enchanting."

Malach From Hebrew, meaning "angel" or "messenger." *Malachi*, meaning "my angel," is a minor prophet in the Bible.

Malki From Hebrew, meaning "my king." Variants: *Malkiel* "God is my king"), *Malkiram* ("God is mighty"), *Malkishu'a* ("God—or my king—is salvation"), *Malki-Tzedek* ("my king is justice).

Malkosh From Hebrew, meaning "last rainfall of the year."

Malon From Hebrew, meaning "a resting place."

Mano'ach From Hebrew. In the Bible he is listed as Samson's father.

Manor From Hebrew, meaning "weaver's beam."

Ma'on From Hebrew. An ancient city mentioned in the Bible.

Ma'or From Hebrew, meaning "light." Boys and girls born during the Chanukah season are often given this name.

Marnin From Hebrew, meaning "producing joy."

Ma'oz From Hebrew, meaning "fortress" or "strength." Variant: *Ma'ozya*, meaning "God's strength."

Margo'a From Hebrew, meaning "resting place."

Marom From Hebrew, meaning "exalted."

Mashi'ach From Hebrew, meaning "the Messiah." A name usually found only among Sephardic families.

Maskil From Hebrew, meaning "intellectual."

Masos From Hebrew, meaning "gladness, joyfulness."

Matan From Hebrew, meaning "gift." Variant: *Mataniah*, meaning "God's gift."

Matar From Hebrew, meaning "rainfall."

Matzli'ach From Hebrew, meaning "successful." A popular name among Sephardic families.

Matityahu From Hebrew, meaning "gift of God." An activist priest and patriot, two centuries B.C., whose five sons were the Maccabees. English equivalents: *Mathew, Mattathias*.

Matmon From Hebrew, meaning "a treasure."

Mazor From Hebrew, meaning "medicine."

Max From Latin, meaning "great, famous." Once a very popular name among Jews, now making a comeback. Akin to *Maximilian, Maxim, Maxwell*.

Mazal From Hebrew, meaning "star" or "luck."

Mechubad From Hebrew, meaning "respected person."

Meged From Hebrew, meaning "precious thing."

Mehadar From Hebrew, meaning "excellent, pleasant."

Mehulal From Hebrew, meaning "one who is praised, adored."

Me'ir From Hebrew, meaning "one who brings light."

Meitar From Hebrew, meaning "string" or "cord." Used also for girls.

Melitz From Hebrew, meaning "advisor, advocate."

Menachem From Hebrew, meaning "comforter." Used often for boys born during the Hebrew month of Av, recalling the destruction of the Temples.

Menashe From Hebrew. Joseph's son. Popular English version: *Manasseh*.

Meretz From Hebrew, meaning "energetic."

Meron From Hebrew, meaning "troops" or "sheep." Mount Meron, in the Galilee, is a revered holy site.

Meshubach From Hebrew, meaning "lauded" or "superior."

Meshulam From Hebrew, meaning "perfect, complete." Mentioned in the Bible.

Metushelach From Hebrew. Better known in English as Methuselah, the oldest person ever, who died at the age of 999.

Mevaser-Tov From Hebrew, meaning "messenger of good tidings."

Mevorach From Hebrew, meaning "blessed."

Meydad From Hebrew, meaning "friend." A leader during Moses' time.

Micha From Hebrew, an acronym for "Who is like unto God," Variants: *Michiyah*, *Michiyahu*.

Michael From Hebrew, meaning "Who is like God." Michael is regarded as the prince of God's angels. Variant: *Mitchell*, *Michel*. Nicknames: *Mike*, *Mikey*, *Muki*.

Migdal From Hebrew, meaning "tower."

Miklot From Hebrew, meaning "sprout" or "palm tree."

Misgav From Hebrew, meaning "stronghold."

Mishan From Hebrew, meaning "support."

Mishlat From Hebrew, meaning "commanding ground."

Mishmar From Hebrew, meaning "guard."

Mitzhal From Hebrew, meaning "joy."

Mivtach From Hebrew, meaning "faith, confidence."

Mivtzar From Hebrew, meaning "stronghold."

Mo'adya From Hebrew, meaning "assembly of God."

Molada From Hebrew, meaning "homeland."

Moran From Hebrew, meaning "teacher."

Mordecai From Persian, possibly meaning "follower of Marduk (a Babylonian god)." Cousin and guardian of Esther, the hero of the biblical book which bears her name. Boys born on Purim are often given this name. Nicknames: *Muttel*, *Mord'che* (Yiddish), *Motti*, *Motke* (in Israel).

Moriel From Hebrew, meaning "God is my teacher."

Moshe From Hebrew, meaning "drawn from water," referring to how baby Moses was saved. Very popular name universally. English variants: *Morris*, *Maurice*, *Murray*. Actually, Morris and Murray are of Greek and Latin origin, meaning "dark skinned," but have always been popular with Jews.

Motza From Hebrew, meaning "source." Mentioned in the Bible.

𝔑

Na'ari From Hebrew, meaning "my boy."

Nachman From Hebrew, meaning "comforter." Variant: *Nachum*.

Nadav From Hebrew, meaning "generous, princely."

Na'eh From Hebrew, meaning "handsome."

Naftali From Hebrew, meaning "one who wrestles," referring to Jacob's bout with the angel.

Nagid From Hebrew, meaning "ruler, prince."

Nagiv From Hebrew, meaning "southward," that means toward the Negev in the south of Israel.

Nahor From Aramaic, meaning "light."

Naim From Hebrew, meaning "sweet, pleasant." Variant: *No'am*.

Namer From Hebrew, meaning "leopard" or "tiger."

Nasi From Hebrew, meaning "leader."

Natan From Hebrew, meaning "gift." A biblical prophet. Variant spelling: *Nathan*.

Nathaniel From Hebrew, meaning "gift of God." Variant spelling: *Nathanael*.

Nativ From Hebrew, meaning "path."

Navon From Hebrew, meaning "wise."

Neal From Gaelic, meaning "courageous person." Although not of Jewish origin, this name has become popular among Jews. Variant: *Neil*.

Nechemiah From Hebrew, meaning "comforted by God." Variant spelling: *Nehemiah*. Nickname: *Chemi*.

Ne'eman From Hebrew, meaning "faithful."

Negev From Hebrew, name of the desert in southern Israel.

Ner From Hebrew, meaning "light" or "candle."

Nerli From Hebrew, meaning "my light."

Nes From Hebrew, meaning "miracle."

Nesher From Hebrew, meaning "eagle."

Netanya From Hebrew, meaning "gift of the Lord."

Nili A Hebrew acronym, taken from the Bible: "The eternity of Israel is not false." Also, a nickname for *Neal* and *Neil*.

Nir From Hebrew, meaning "to plow."

Nisim From Hebrew, meaning "miracles."

Nissan From Hebrew, meaning "emblem." Also a spring month in the Jewish calendar.

Niv From Aramaic, meaning "expression."

Noah From Hebrew, meaning "restfulness." He and his immediate family, and his animal passengers, survived the flood. Variant spelling: *Noach*.

No'am See *Naim*.

No'da From Hebrew, meaning "famous."

Noga From Hebrew, meaning "bright." One of King David's sons. Also used for girls.

Noy From Hebrew, meaning "beauty."

Nur From Aramaic, meaning "fire." Variant: *Nuriel*, meaning "fire of God."

Obadiah From Hebrew, meaning "God's servant." A minor prophet, whose book in the Bible consists of only one chapter. Variant: *Ovadiah*.

Oded From Hebrew, meaning "to restore." A prophet in the days of King Ahaz.

Ofer From Hebrew, meaning "young deer."

Ofir From Hebrew, meaning "gold." Variant spelling: *Ophir*.

Ofra From Hebrew, meaning "young mountain goat."

Ogen From Hebrew, meaning "anchor" or "binding."

Omen From Hebrew, meaning "loyal, faithful."

Ometz From Hebrew, meaning "strength."

Omri From Hebrew, meaning "bundle of harvested wheat." Also from Arabic, meaning "my life." He is listed in the Bible as a king of Israel.

Or From Hebrew, meaning "light." Variant: *Ori,* meaning "my light."

Oran From Aramaic, meaning "light."

Oren From Hebrew, meaning "pine tree."

Oshaya From Hebrew, meaning "helped by God."

Otniel From Hebrew, meaning "God is my strength."

Ozni From Hebrew, meaning "my hearing." A son of Gad. Nickname: *Oz*.

P

Pagiel From Hebrew, meaning "to pray."

Paltiel From Hebrew, meaning "my deliverance." King Saul's son-in-law.

Papa From Aramaic. A great talmudic scholar during the Babylonian exile. Variants: *Papai*, *Papos*.

Pardes From Hebrew, meaning "citrus orchard."

Parnas From Hebrew, meaning "leader" or "supporter."

Patish From Hebrew, meaning "a hammer." Talmudic scholar in ancient Israel.

Paz From Hebrew, meaning "gold, golden," Used also for girls.

Pe'er From Hebrew, meaning "glory" or "beauty."

Pekach From Hebrew, meaning "to blossom." In biblical days, a king of Israel.

Peled From Hebrew, meaning "iron."

Peleh From Hebrew, meaning "wonder, miracle."

P'ri From Hebrew, meaning "fruit."

Peri'el From Hebrew, meaning "fruit of the Lord."

Pesach The Hebrew term for Passover. Boys born during this holiday are often given this name.

Pinchas From Hebrew, meaning "snake's mouth." In the Bible he is the grandson of Aaron, the High Priest, and is himself a priest. In Egyptian tradition, the name means "dark-complexioned." Variant: *Phineas.* Nickname: *Pinky.*

Putiel From Aramaic, meaning "servant of God." He was the father-in-law of Elazar, Aaron's son in the Bible.

ℜ

Ra'amya From Hebrew, meaning "God's thunder."

Ra'anan From Hebrew, meaning "luxuriant."

Racham From Hebrew, meaning "compassion." A descendant of Judah, in the Bible. Variant: *Rachamim*, a popular name among Sephardic Jews.

Rachmiel From Hebrew, meaning "God's compassion." A shortened version of *Yerachmiel.*

Rafa From Hebrew, meaning "healing." Benjamin's descendant, in the Bible.

Ranan From Hebrew, meaning "to rejoice" or "to sing." Variant: *Ranon.*

Raphael From Hebrew, meaning "God has healed." In Jewish tradition, the angel Raphael stands directly behind God.

Rava From Hebrew, meaning "great" or "teacher."

Raviv From Hebrew, meaning "rain" or "dew."

Raziel From Aramaic, meaning "God's secret."

Rechavam From Hebrew, meaning "the people's expanse" or "freedom." In the Bible, he is King Solomon's son who succeeds him on the throne.

Remez From Hebrew, meaning "omen, sign."

Reuben From Hebrew, literally meaning "Look—a son!" He was Jacob's first-born son, by his wife Leah, and founder of one of the Twelve Tribes of Israel. Variant: *Reuven.*

Reu'el From Hebrew, meaning "friend of God." It is the alternative name of Moses' father-in-law, Jethro.

Rimon From Hebrew, meaning "pomegranate." It also refers to the ornaments—usually made of silver—that are affixed to the Torah scroll when it is carried around the synagogue at services.

Ron From Hebrew, meaning "song" or "my song." Nickname: *Ronnie*. Variant: *Ronli*.

Saba From Hebrew and Aramaic, meaning "aged" or "grandpa."

Sa'adya From Hebrew, meaning "God's helper." Often a scholar's name.

Safra From Aramaic, meaning "writer." A famous talmudic scholar.

Sagi From Aramaic, meaning "strong, mighty."

Samson From Hebrew, meaning "the sun." The biblical account of Samson the Mighty is well-known; he was also a judge, and fought against the Philistines, until Delilah cut his hair. Variant spelling: *Sampson*.

Samuel From Hebrew, meaning "his name is God" or "God heard." A prophet and a judge in ancient Israel, he anointed the first king of Israel, Saul.

Sapir From Hebrew, meaning "precious stone," usually translated as a sapphire.

Saul From Hebrew, meaning "he asked" or "he borrowed." Israel's first king who eventually became David's mortal enemy.

Segel From Hebrew, meaning "a treasure."

Segev From Hebrew, meaning "glory."

Seled From Hebrew, meaning "to leap for joy." A member of Judah's tribe.

Sela From Hebrew, meaning "a rock."

Selig From German and Yiddish, meaning "blessed soul."

Senior From Latin, meaning "elder." Popular Yiddish variant: *Shneur*.

Seriel From Hebrew, meaning "God's prince." Nickname form of the name *Yisrael*.

Setav From Hebrew, meaning "autumn." Variant: *S'tav*.

Seth From Hebrew, meaning "appointed." Adam and Eve's son, born after the murder of Abel; so named because God "appointed" another seed.

Sha'arya From Hebrew, meaning "gate of the Lord."

Shabtai From Aramaic, meaning "Sabbath rest." The name appears in the Bible and in the Talmud; and

although it was the name of a "false messiah," it remains popular in the Sephardic community.

Shachar From Hebrew, meaning "dawn."

Shadmon From Hebrew, meaning "farm" or "vineyard."

Shai From Hebrew, meaning "gift." Also a nickname form of *Isaiah*.

Shalev From Hebrew, meaning "peaceful, secure."

Shalom From Hebrew, meaning "peace."

Shamir From Hebrew. Mentioned in the Bible, it is a strong rock-like substance that can cut metal. Sometimes translated as "diamond."

Shammai From Aramaic and Hebrew, meaning "name." A famous scholar noted for his rigid interpretations of the Bible, unlike Hillel who was much more flexible.

Shanan From Hebrew, meaning "secure." Variant spelling: *Sha'anan*.

Shapir From Aramaic, meaning "beautiful." It is believed that the popular surname Shapiro stems from this name.

She'altiel From Hebrew, meaning "borrowed from God." Variant: *Shaltiel*.

Shevach From Hebrew, meaning "praise" or "fame."

Shikmon From Hebrew, meaning "sycamore tree."

Shmarya From Hebrew, meaning "God's protection." Yiddish nickname form: *Shmerel*.

Shmelke From Yiddish, nickname form of *Shmu'el*, the Hebrew form of *Samuel*.

Shofar From Hebrew, meaning "horn" or "trumpet."

Shofet From Hebrew, meaning "judge."

Shomer From Hebrew, meaning "sentry."

Shefer From Hebrew, meaning "pleasant."

Sherira From Aramaic, meaning "strong." In modern Hebrew, it means "muscle."

Shneur From Yiddish, meaning "elder," A name popular with the Hassidic Jews.

Shraga From Aramaic, meaning "light." Variant: *Shragai*.

Siman Tov From Hebrew, meaning "good omen, good luck."

Simcha From Hebrew, meaning "joy."

Simeon From Hebrew, meaning "to hear" or "to be heard." One of Jacob's twelve sons and the founder

of one of the Twelve Tribes of Israel. Variant: *Simon*. Nicknames: *Si, Shimmel*.

Sinai From Hebrew. A figurative term given to a very great talmudic scholar, Yosef bar-Chiya, because of his extensive memory.

Sivan From Hebrew. The ninth month in the Jewish calender. It usually falls in May or June.

Sisi From Hebrew, meaning "rejoice!" or "my joy."

Solomon From Hebrew. King Solomon, the son of King David, was known for building the Temple in Jerusalem, and for his great intellect. His name in Hebrew, *Shlomo*, refers to peace. Three books of the Bible are attributed to him: Proverbs, Song of Songs, and Ecclesiastes. Variant. *Shelomi*.

Tachan From Hebrew, meaning "prayer."

Tachash From Hebrew, meaning "dolphin" or "ocean seal." Also the name of Abraham's nephew.

Tachkemoni From Hebrew, meaning "change." Also a famous talmudic scholar in Babylon.

Tal From Hebrew, meaning "dew." Used also for girls.

Talia From Aramaic, meaning 'young lamb." Used also for girls.

Talmai From Hebrew, meaning "mound." Also King David's father-in-law.

Talor From Hebrew, meaning "morning dew."

Tam From Hebrew, meaning "honest" or "whole."

Tamir From Hebrew, meaning "stately like a palm tree."

Tanchum From Hebrew, meaning "consoler, comforter." Also a talmudic scholar in Babylon.

Tanna From Aramaic, meaning "teacher."

Tavi From Aramaic, meaning "good." Variant: *Tabai*.

Tavas From Hebrew, meaning "peacock."

Tikva From Hebrew, meaning "hope." Used also for girls.

Tivon From Hebrew, meaning "student of nature."

Timur From Hebrew, meaning "stately."

Tov From Hebrew, meaning "good." Believed to be related to the names *Tobiah* and *Tobias*.

Tuviah From Hebrew, meaning "God is good."

Mentioned in the Bible. Variants: *Toviah*,
Toby, *Tobias*.

Tzadik From Hebrew, meaning "righteous person." Akin
to *Tzadok*, *Zadok*.

Tzahal From Hebrew, meaning "shout of joy." Also
acronym for the Israel Defense Forces.

Tzefaniah From Hebrew, meaning "hidden or guarded by
God." One of the Bible's minor prophets. Variant
spelling: *Zephaniah*.

Tzvi From Hebrew, meaning "deer." Variant spelling: *Zvi*.
Variant: *Tzevi*.

U

Ud From Hebrew, meaning "firebrand." Also a nickname
for *Ehud*. Variant: *Udi*.

Upaz From Hebrew, meaning "gold."

Uri From Hebrew, meaning "my light."

Uriah From Hebrew, meaning "God's light." Variant:
Uriel. In Jewish tradition, he is one of the four angels
ministering in God's presence.

Uza From Hebrew, meaning "strength." Also the name of a bud.

Uzi From Hebrew, meaning "my strength."

Uziyahu From Hebrew, meaning "God is my strength." Historically, he was king of Judah. Variants: *Uziyah*, *Uziel*.

Velvel Yiddish form of *William*.

Vered From Hebrew, meaning "a rose."

Vivien English equivalent to the Hebrew name *Chaim*, meaning "life." Used as a boy's name primarily in Britain. Variant: *Vivian*.

Y

Yaacov Hebrew form of *Jacob*.

Ya'al From Hebrew, meaning "to ascend."

Ya'azanya From Hebrew, meaning "God will listen." Variant: *Ya'aziyahu*.

Yabetz A biblical place name. Variant: *Yavetz*.

Yachaziel From Hebrew, meaning "God sees." Also a priest in King David's time.

Yadid From Hebrew, meaning "friend" or "beloved." Variant spelling: *Yedid*.

Yadin From Hebrew, meaning "he will judge." Variant: *Yadon*.

Yagel From Hebrew, meaning "he will reveal."

Ya'ir From Hebrew, meaning "he will enlighten." In the Bible, he is Joseph's grandson.

Ya'ish From Hebrew, designating a constellation of stars.

Yakir From Hebrew, meaning "precious" or "beloved."

Yankel Yiddish nickname for *Yaacov, Jacob*, or *Jack*.

Yarkon From Hebrew, meaning "green." Also a small bird that appears in Israel during the summer. Also a small river near Tel Aviv.

Yashar From Hebrew, meaning "upright" or "honorable."

Yavin From Hebrew, meaning "he will understand." Listed in the Bible as a Canaanite king.

Yavniel From Hebrew, meaning "God will build."

Yechiel From Hebrew, meaning "may God live." In the Bible, an ancestor of Gershon.

Yediel From Hebrew, meaning "knowing the Lord." Biblical variant: *Yedia-El*.

Yehiam From Hebrew, meaning "may the people live."

Yehudah Hebrew name of *Judah*, Jacob's son and founder of one of the Twelve Tribes of Israel. When the Ten Lost Tribes in the northern part of Israel were captured, presumably enslaved and eventually disappeared into history, only Judah and the small tribe of Benjamin survived. Nowadays all Jews are descended from Judah.

Yekutiel From Hebrew, meaning "God will provide."

Yerachmiel From Hebrew, meaning "God's mercy." A son of King Jehoiakim of Judah. Variant: *Rachmiel*.

Yeshurun From Hebrew, meaning "upright." A synonym used to designate the Jewish people.

Yiftach From Hebrew, meaning "he will open." A biblical judge.

Yigal From Hebrew, meaning "he will redeem." The name appears in the Bible several times. Variants: *Igal*, *Yigael*.

Yigdal From Hebrew, meaning "he will grow."

Yoav From Hebrew, meaning "God is father." Biblically, he was King David's nephew.

Yochanan From Hebrew, meaning "gracious."

Yoel From Hebrew, meaning "God is willing." This is the Hebrew name of *Joel*, a minor prophet in the Bible. Yiddish nickname form: *Yale*.

Yona From Hebrew, meaning "dove."

Yora From Hebrew, meaning "to teach." A biblical name.

Yoram From Hebrew, meaning "God is exalted." The name appears in the Bible. Variant: *Yehoram*.

Yudan From Hebrew, meaning "he will be judged."

Z

Zak From Hebrew, nickname for Isaac. Variant: *Zaki*.

Zachariah From Hebrew, meaning "remembrance of God." In the Bible, one Zachariah is a prophet, another is a king of Israel. Variant spelling: *Zechariah*. Nickname: *Zak*.

Zakkai From Hebrew, meaning "pure, innocent." One of the greatest Jewish leaders and scholars was Johanan ben Zakkai. The name was taken by a family that returned to Jerusalem from Babylonian exile.

Zalman A Yiddish form of *Solomon*.

Zamir From Hebrew, meaning "song" or "nightingale."

Zavdi From Hebrew, meaning "my gift" or "my gift is God." The father of one of King David's officers bore that name. Variants: *Zavdiel*.

Zedekiah From Hebrew, meaning "God is righteousness." Also the name of a king of Judah.

Zehavi From Hebrew, meaning "golden." Used for girls and boys.

Zemirah From Hebrew, meaning "song." Mentioned in the Bible. In the plural, "zemiros" or "zemirot" are Sabbath table songs.

Zemariah From Hebrew, meaning "song of God."

Zemer From Hebrew, meaning "melody."

Zephaniah From Hebrew. A minor prophet in the Bible, scion of a noble family.

Zera From Aramaic, meaning "small, tiny."

Zerubavel From Hebrew, meaning "Babylonian exile."

Zev From Hebrew, meaning "wolf." The usual Hebrew equivalent name for *William*.

Zevadiah From Hebrew, meaning "God's gift." Listed in the Bible a number of times.

Zeviel From Hebrew, meaning "God's gazelle."

Zevulun From Hebrew. One of Jacob's twelve sons, and the founder of a tribe bearing that name. The name is generally associated with the sea. Variant: *Zebulun*.

Zichroni From Hebrew, meaning "my remembrance."

Zimri From Hebrew, meaning "mountain sheep" or "goat." It also means a sacred object." Variant: *Zimran*.

Zindel A Yiddish version of "sonny boy."

Zion From Hebrew, literally meaning "excellent." Also meaning "sign." Synonymous for Israel or Jerusalem. Hebrew pronunciation: *Tziyon*.

Ziv From Hebrew, meaning "brilliance." Also a synonym for the Hebrew month of Iyar, which usually falls in May.

JUDAICA TITLES
FROM HIPPOCRENE

1,301 QUESTIONS AND ANSWERS ABOUT JUDAISM
David C. Gross
448 pages • 6 x 9 • 0-7818-0578-3 • W • $17.95pb • (678)

UNDER THE WEDDING CANOPY:
LOVE AND MARRIAGE IN JUDAISM
David C. Gross and Esther R. Gross
243 pages • 5½ x 8¼ • 0-7818-0481-7 • W • $22.50hc • (596)

DICTIONARY OF 1,000 JEWISH PROVERBS
David C. Gross
131 pages • 5½ x 8½ • 0-7818-0529-5 • W • $11.95pb • (628)

TREASURY OF JEWISH LOVE POEMS,
QUOTATIONS AND PROVERBS
128 pages • 5 x 7 • 0-7818-0308-X • $11.95hc • (346)
AUDIO CASSETTE: 0-7818-0363-2 • $12.95 • (579)

All prices are subject to change without prior notice. To order Hippocrene Books, contact your local bookstore, call (718) 454-2366, or write to: Hippocrene Books, 171 Madison Avenue, New York, NY 10016. Please enclose check or money order adding $5.00 shipping (UPS) for the first book and $.50 for each additional title.